First Mistake

Facing Death, Finding Life

by D.J. Chang

Cover illustration by C.R. Hammons

Published by Equity Incites Press, Wellington, NV in Association with Best Seller Publishing®, Pasadena, CA
Best Seller Publishing® is a registered trademark
Printed in the United States of America.
ISBN 978-1-946978-83-7

This publication is designed to provide accurate and authoritative information with regard to the subject matter covered. It is sold with the understanding that the publisher is not engaged in rendering legal, accounting, or other professional advice. If legal advice or other expert assistance is required, the services of a competent professional should be sought. The opinions expressed by the authors in this book are not endorsed by Best Seller Publishing® and are the sole responsibility of the author rendering the opinion.

Most Best Seller Publishing® titles are available at special quantity discounts for bulk purchases for sales promotions, premiums, fundraising, and educational use. Special versions or book excerpts can also be created to fit specific needs.

For more information, please write:
Best Seller Publishing®
1346 Walnut Street, #205
Pasadena, CA 91106
or call 1(626) 765 9750
Toll Free: 1(844) 850-3500

Visit us online at: www.BestSellerPublishing.org

Table of Contents

Dedication

To my beautiful wife, whose incredible strength and support has made everything in my life possible and made me believe in miracles.

To all our furry babies, present and past, who have so enriched our lives.

And to my creator as well as my spirit guide, Ah Kung, who taught me about unconditional love, faith, and purpose.

Disclaimer

The events, locales, and conversations described in this memoir are from my memories of them. In order to maintain their privacy and anonymity, in some instances I have changed the names and identifying characteristics of individuals, organizations, and places.

Epigraph

So when the woman saw that the tree was good for food, and that it was a delight to the eyes, and the tree was to be desired to make one wise, she took of its fruit and ate; and she also gave some to her husband, who was with her, and he ate. Then the eyes of both were opened...

GENESIS 3:6–7

Introduction

I started talking to Ah Kung a few weeks after his death. My hope was that, being a spirit, he would be able to help me keep from making mistakes in my life. Sadly, that expectation was just wishful thinking.

Talking to Ah Kung after his death may be even more surprising than you'd think because the two of us never communicated when he was alive—at least not with words. He had been a servant to my grandfather back in China, decades before I was born. He accompanied my father and his family when they moved to America and, though Ah Kung lived in this country for more than thirty years, he never learned to speak English. I, on the other hand, was born here and learned no Chinese while growing up. Ah Kung lived with us until I was almost nine, but throughout that time, he and I never spoke.

Then he died.

After that, language was no longer a barrier between us. Suddenly I was able to hear all the things that I imagined he used to say to me through his loving and concerned eyes. And I've been listening to his voice ever since.

But did it help me avoid mistakes?

One look at my life now, and the answer becomes pretty clear. Today my life is a complicated mess. I'm out of work, running out of money, and my house is in complete disarray. I eat too much or forget to eat, have trouble sleeping or can't stay awake. I'm scared of dying but sometimes more scared of living. My plans or ambitions seem like extraordinary fantasies or delusions. Or else I find myself with no real plans at all. In short, I don't know what I'm doing.

I could have chosen to do it all differently—could have steadfastly avoided complications and taken an easier route. In fact, there was a time when I thought that living a normal, uncomplicated life was all I wanted. But later, as I found myself confronting choices, my intractable yearnings led me elsewhere. Instead of staying clear of obstacles, I almost sought them out. It was as if my conversations with Ah Kung gave me the courage to do things that more practical people would avoid.

I'm not saying that it was Ah Kung's fault, mind you. He never told me what to do. He just kept asking me what was going on in my head and heart during my journey to this place. All along, I thought I'd been doing a good job answering Ah Kung's questions, and I was convinced that with Ah Kung's help, I could lead a life free from mistakes.

Instead, this is what happened.

PART I

Forming Me

CHAPTER I

Please breathe, Ah Kung (My First Mistake)

Ah Kung died of a heart attack right under my hands. It was a summer evening, about a month before my ninth birthday. At the age of eighty-six and retired from his life-long career as a domestic servant, Ah Kung lived with us and occasionally babysat when my parents went out. He had just cleaned off the dinner table, and my brother Martin and I were settled in front of the TV to watch the movie of the week on *The Wonderful World of Disney*. *Pollyanna* was playing that night. Ah Kung positioned himself on a swiveling, black vinyl bar stool next to the TV in order to keep his eye on Martin and me. My first reaction when I saw Ah Kung fall to the floor was to laugh.

I thought he was getting back at me for all the times I'd fake a fall and pretend to get hurt, just so I could laugh at him when he came to my rescue unnecessarily. A few days earlier, while Ah Kung was busy chopping vegetables in the kitchen for our evening meal, I had tumbled down the staircase leading to our front door. When I reached the bottom in a noisy crash, I pretended to cry—and even managed to squeeze out a few glistening crocodile tears while I waited for Ah Kung to come. I lay motionless on the landing with my arms cradling my head, pretending to scream in pain. In the narrow space between my arms I could see Ah Kung as he hurriedly shuffled over to the top of the stairs to see if I was all right. I saw the worried look in his eyes, accentuated by his bushy eyebrows, which had grown long on him in his old age and pointed up at the ends. He held onto the railing to steady himself and slowly rocked down the stairs, shifting his weight from one foot on one stair and then to the other on a lower step, his knees barely bending during the descent. As I waited for him to reach me, I took another deep breath to continue my wailing. When Ah Kung made it to the landing, a faint groan escaped his mouth as he bent down to touch the higher of my two arms. Then he asked me something in Chinese. I waited another few seconds for effect before I burst out laughing as loudly as I had pretended to cry. Ah Kung reached for the bottom curl of the railing to help himself straighten up. With his other hand, he patted me on the head and his look of worry turned into a reluctant, but amused smile. "Ah, Sya Meh!" he said. He always called me "Sya Meh," meaning "little sister." I smiled back, pleased that I had gotten him again.

I often played tricks like that on Ah Kung. Early on, I realized that I could get away with a lot of mischief and not only would Ah Kung not tell my parents, but he'd almost always help cover up my misdeed. I could leave my things lying around the house knowing that Ah Kung would pick up after me—usually before my mother had a chance to find them. One time though when I was about three, I left one of my toys, a musical keyboard that blew up balloons when you pushed down on the keys, on a step in the middle of the staircase. Ah Kung hadn't found it yet when my mother slipped on it and fell down the stairs. She fractured her knee and had to get a pin implanted to hold the joint together. That incident and the operation that followed were so painful for my mother that she opted out of a second operation and never got the pin removed. My father firmly scolded me for not picking up after myself and causing the accident. After that, Ah Kung kept a closer watch on me to make sure he wouldn't miss anything I might leave behind.

When Ah Kung fell off his stool that night, it took me several seconds before I noticed the blood dripping from the side of his mouth and the swelling bump over his right eye. I nearly choked on my laugh when I realized he wasn't playing a joke.

Martin, who's three years older than me, pushed me aside to kneel next to Ah Kung on the kitchen floor. He helped Ah Kung lie lengthwise on his back. "Stay with him," Martin ordered softly. "I'll go call for help." I watched Martin make his way to my parents' bedroom down the hall on the opposite side of the house before crawling on my hands and knees to be next to Ah Kung. His eyes were closed and his teeth were clenched, almost as if he were smiling. I watched him closely. He wasn't trying to move at all and, from the look of his slowly rising and falling stomach, he was barely breathing. I had read somewhere (or maybe saw something on TV) about mouth-to-mouth resuscitation but didn't really know how to perform it. Besides, the blood leaking out of the corner of his mouth scared me and I couldn't bring myself to bring my own mouth anywhere near it. Instead, I knelt beside him and pushed down on his stomach, hoping that the pressure would help him breathe better. I pushed only once and felt his stomach go down with the weight of my hands.

"Breathe... breathe... *please* breathe, Ah Kung." But when I lifted my hands back up, his stomach stayed flat like a deflated football. I got scared and ran back to be with Martin.

"What's taking so long?" I complained.

"Shush," my brother answered, as he wrote down a number on a pad of paper. There were two other numbers above the one he had just written. "They keep giving me different numbers to call," he explained after hanging up. He dialed the third number and waited for an answer.

"Yes, thank you," he began in his most serious and responsible voice. He sounded older than twelve.

"My sister and I are home with our babysitter and he just collapsed. I think he had a heart attack. Can you send someone to the house to help us?" I stayed with Martin as he explained about Ah Kung's age and condition and gave the person on the line our address.

"They're going to send firemen to the house," he explained to me.

I thought of the TV show *Emergency* and said, "That's neat!" Martin looked at me oddly and I felt stupid for my excited outburst.

Martin stayed with me in my parents' bedroom waiting for the fire truck to arrive. I was grateful that he didn't ask me why I had run to him rather than staying with Ah Kung. I didn't want to tell him about what had happened when I pushed on Ah Kung's stomach. Instead, Martin got a book called *Rags* to read to me. It was about a dog. His voice was calm and rhythmic as he read.

When the doorbell rang, Martin finished the sentence he was reading. Then he handed me the book. "I have to go talk to the firemen. Will you be okay back here?"

I remembered the way Ah Kung had looked and how his stomach had felt under my hands. "Yeah, I'll finish reading the book," I told him.

I was still sitting on my parents' bed staring at the book when a young fireman, dressed in full gear, gingerly entered my parents' bedroom. "Your brother says you have a neighbor you can stay with while we're… taking care of things here. And until your parents get home." The fireman escorted my brother and me to our neighbor's house. We had to pass the kitchen to get to the front door. I only peeked quickly over at where I had left Ah Kung. There were a couple of firemen around him and a stretcher leaning up against the refrigerator. I looked up at our escort's face, but it revealed no explanation. We reached our neighbor's house that was two houses clockwise from ours in the court where we lived. Our neighbors were a French family of four and they all still spoke English with an accent. Auntie Monique—she wasn't really our aunt, but my parents had us call all of their friends "auntie" or "uncle"—opened the door. The young fireman asked me to remain by the front door while he and my brother spoke to Auntie Monique. I guessed what they were telling her but waited patiently by the door. From where I stood, I smelled the familiar fragrance of our neighbors' house. It always smelled like freshly baked bread and something or other sautéed with butter.

The fireman excused himself, and Auntie Monique invited us inside. She told us that her daughter, who was only about five, was already in bed and that Uncle Fabrice was working in his study. Their son, Henri, was in the basement watching TV. She suggested that we join him.

As we descended the stairs to the basement, Auntie Monique called to us, "Can you ask Henri to come upstairs for a moment?"

Henri turned with surprise as he saw us. "What are you doing here?" he asked in his odd accent.

"Something happened to Ah Kung," I explained. "So, we're going to stay with you until our parents get home."

Henri bounded up the stairs when I told him that his mother wanted to see him. Martin and I sat down on the Persian carpet in front of their TV. It seemed strange to me that *Pollyanna* was playing here too. Henri bounced back down the stairs after a few minutes and joined us in front of the TV. I couldn't concentrate on the story though, as I kept thinking what had just happened at our house.

Ah Kung was always a good protector to me. In China, he had served my father's family, but in America, he worked as a paid domestic for a wealthy Chinese family in Yonkers (since my grandparents no longer had money to keep him) until around the age of seventy, when he retired and came to live with us. But living in my parents' home, Ah Kung was not afraid to voice his opinions. I never understood what he said, but I always got the gist from how he said it. Ah Kung was never disrespectful to either of my parents (it's hard to break old habits of servitude) but I always knew that he was on my side. Ah Kung was the one I looked to for comfort when my parents were disappointed in me.

I remembered how I turned to Ah Kung one day when I was about five. My mother and I were passing the time while my brother was taking piano lessons. My mother was holding open the book *Are You My Mother?* She was trying to teach me to read.

I pointed to a small word with my finger. "Tuh-huh-eh," I said.

"What?" my mother demanded.

"Tuh-huh-eh," I repeated slowly.

"How can you know the word 'mother' and not be able to read 'THE?'" I thought I saw everyone in the waiting room turn to glare at us. It seemed to me that her voice was much louder than it had to be. She shut the book in disgust, then took out a smaller but much thicker book from her purse and began reading it silently to herself.

When we got home, my mother instructed me to take my book into my room and not to come out until I could read it aloud from front to back. I grabbed the book and ran to Ah Kung. Ah Kung furrowed his brow and questioned my mother in Chinese. My mother answered him. My guess was that she was telling him how stupid I was. Ah Kung let me linger with him for a moment and bury my face in his pant leg. Then he gently patted the hair just above my neck, guiding me to my room and saying something that made me feel better. Looking up at Ah Kung's eyes, I knew he took my side.

My seclusion with the book that afternoon helped me learn to read. I suppose I owed that to my mother. But what I was really grateful for was Ah Kung's comfort. He knew I wasn't deliberately trying to provoke my mother by acting stupid. It was just a silly mistake and he forgave me for it. But could he forgive me for leaving him alone on the floor? I was angry that I let my fear pull me away from him when he needed me most. And I realized that I probably shouldn't have pressed down on his stomach. I wished I hadn't been so afraid of the blood so I could have given him mouth-to-mouth instead of pushing on him the way I did. I was family to him since he had left his own back in China. Ah Kung had a wife and daughter from an arranged marriage, but he never returned to China to be reunited with them. His other family had been chosen for him, but I was part of the family he chose for himself. He was as good to me as any grandparent could be, and closer to me than my real ones. I knew I had let him down.

At one of the commercial breaks, Henri turned to me and asked, "So the firemen came to take Ah Kung's body away?"

"They came to help him."

"Ah Kung's dead, you know," Henri offered arrogantly.

Henri was a year younger than I. He was a couple of inches taller, but skinny. I thought I could take him down with a punch to the face. But I just bit my lip and stayed silent. I knew he was telling the truth.

Our parents arrived at our neighbor's house before the movie ended. My father looked upset. He came over to Martin and me where we sat, hugged us, and asked if we were all right.

"Can we just go home?" I wanted to ask him if Ah Kung was dead. But I didn't want Henri to have the satisfaction of hearing the answer.

"Yes, Ah Kung died," my father explained to me when we got home. "He was very old you know and had heart problems. I'm so sorry you had to be alone with him when it happened."

The pain in my father's voice made me cry. I noticed tears beginning to form in his eyes, too, and I remembered that Ah Kung had also raised my father.

"What's going to happen to Ah Kung now?" I asked.

"Well, his body is being sent to a funeral home. There will be a service and then we'll bury him. I think there also ought to be a service at the temple he used to always go to. I'll talk to the monks about it tomorrow."

"Oh." I was hoping for another kind of answer.

"Do you think you want to go to the funeral?" he asked.

"Sure," I answered, still distracted.

In the solitude of my room, it was hard for me to sleep. Ah Kung had made my bed that morning. I had gotten up without making it, so he made it for me, as he often did, to ensure I wouldn't get in trouble. I should have made it myself. I didn't even thank him and now I couldn't. But as I lay there, a warm feeling ran through me like a wave, and I sensed that Ah Kung knew I was grateful.

There were so many questions I had wanted to ask my father about Ah Kung's death, but I didn't know how to talk to him about those things. I asked him what was going to happen to Ah Kung now and he told me about the funeral and the memorial service. I didn't know how to explain that I wasn't interested in what would happen to his body. I wanted to know what happened to *him*. Was he just gone now? I wanted to ask about why people die. It seemed unfair to me, like God was playing some kind of cruel joke, giving us life just to take it away. They seemed to be religious questions. But my parents didn't practice any religion and I had only vague notions about God and faith.

Ah Kung, as he aged, became a devout Buddhist. I sensed that he had strong beliefs about right and wrong. He refused to eat or even cook meat (unless it was for my brother and me when my parents were out) and took a bus to New York City almost every weekend to live with the monks at a temple in Chinatown. In his room in the bottom level of our split-level home, he kept and often meditated in front of a shrine that he made from a hollowed-out TV wrapped in aluminum foil. There was a gold-painted "happy" Buddha statue (the fat version) inside the shrine and a small offering bowl that Ah Kung regularly filled with candy bars and fruit. Sometimes, when I noticed a candy bar that I particularly liked, I would sneak into Ah Kung's room and eat it, figuring that the statue wouldn't miss it and couldn't tell on me. Ah Kung never confronted me about my thefts, so I was left to wonder if he was just letting me get away with my mischief again or if maybe he thought that the Buddha had accepted part of his gift. I assumed stealing from Buddha was some kind of sin, so I didn't have much hope that Ah Kung's faith would help me with my questions.

They were all still unanswered by the time Ah Kung's funeral was held a few days later. The funeral was in Chinatown, a few blocks away from the Buddhist temple. I wore my school uniform since it was the only dress I owned at the time. My father took pictures of the funeral in order to send them to his family back in China. My father also sent a note to them telling them that, if they wanted him to, my father would continue to send them money, as Ah Kung had done for all those years. It was an open casket service. The body lying there had no expression, no warmth. It didn't look like the person I loved.

After we buried the casket at some cemetery in Queens, my father drove us back into Chinatown for another Buddhist service at the temple where Ah Kung had spent his weekends. The monks instructed us to each light a stick of incense and place it in a bowl that was positioned in front of a picture of Ah Kung. The incense and our prayers were supposed to help Ah Kung's spirit on its journey. A line of monks had their hands together the way little kids pray at bedtime, and they were rhythmically bowing their heads and chanting a kind of song. Then one of the monks stopped his chant to point at the stick of incense I had lit. It seemed that, while the ash from all the other sticks simply fell off, making little dust piles around them, the ash from my stick remained connected, curling as it lengthened, as if held by some invisible force. The monks at the temple seemed very excited by this strange phenomenon and told me (through my mother's translation) that it must be Ah Kung's spirit promising me that he would always be there for me.

Given how good Ah Kung had been to me in life, it shouldn't have been such a surprise that his spirit kept its promise.

CHAPTER 2

Are You My Mother?

I was always pretty open to things as a kid. Before Ah Kung died, I liked to fool around with Ouija boards and do séances and "levitations" (seeing if a group of about four of us could lift someone by each using only two of our fingers) with my friends. But when I started talking to Ah Kung, I kept it to myself. The first time Ah Kung spoke to me, I was just starting the fourth grade.

"Chinese, Japanese, dirty knees, what are these?" a little boy yelled at me.

The boy had run all the way across the playground to share his little rhyme with me. It came with a series of physical gestures. First, he used the middle fingers of each of his hands to push up the sides of his eyes in an upturned squint: Chinese! Second, he pushed his eyelids downward: Japanese! Then he cupped his kneecaps with each hand: Dirty knees! And finally, he pinched his tee shirt between the fingers of both hands and pulled it outward to mimic breasts: What are these?

I didn't know the boy. He seemed a few years younger than I, but, other than the few kids who lived on my street, I didn't know any of the neighborhood children. My friends were all from the private school I went to in the next town. My mother had left me to wait in the playground across the street from the public high school where she had taken a job as a substitute math teacher. She had forgotten her students' quizzes in her rush to pick me up from school—her class let out at around the same time as my school day ended, and on days she taught, she came late to get me. So, we went back for her to collect the papers for grading. The boy on the playground had short, sandy brown hair and was dressed in blue cotton shorts and a horizontally striped shirt of several different colors. His face was dirty, having just come from roughhousing with a group of boys before running towards me. He caught me just as I finished my ride down the slide. I was trying something new, staying upright, gliding on my leather-soled shoes with my knees tucked under the skirt of my school uniform. I tried to ignore his taunt by calmly walking over to the swing set.

He chased after me, repeating his song and pantomime. I settled myself in the seat of one of the swings, but the boy stood in front of me, blocking me from being able to swing.

"Hey, what are you, Chinese or Japanese? And do you know what these are?" He pinched and pulled his shirt again.

"Go away," I told him. I thought I might scare him away since I was bigger than he. But he didn't back up. I twisted the swing around to face the other direction but lost my footing and the swing spun back around. He had taken a step closer to me so that when I faced him again, my knees were nearly touching him.

"Chinese, I bet," he offered, without any hint of being intimidated. "Ching-chong-chan. That's how you speak, right? Come on, tell me what I'm saying. Ching-chong. Ching-chong. Ching-chong. Ching-chong." He was circling me now and thrashing his arms up and down with each syllable.

"I don't speak Chinese," I told him. "Now leave me alone."

"So, you *are* a ching-chong Chinese," he said, triumphantly.

I remembered a time when my brother and I were both younger. My brother took my mother's advice and told a group of boys that had been teasing him, "Stick and stones may break my bones, but names will never hurt me." The boys took him at his word and threw sticks and stones at him instead. I definitely didn't want to try that line on the boy, so I was relieved when I saw my mother pull up to the curb of the playground in our green station wagon. I ran to the car and jumped into the front seat beside my mother. My mother had long black hair gathered neatly into a ponytail and was sharply dressed. She didn't need to wear any makeup to look attractive. But suddenly the look of her made me angry.

"You're always making me wait places," I complained. "The other mothers pick up their kids on time. I was the last one waiting at school today. And now you made me wait on that stupid playground." My emotions were building up in me and I started to cry.

My mother looked at me with astonishment. "What are you crying about?"

"You. Why can't you be like other mothers?"

"You complain about me? And you think you have a right to cry about such a thing? I tell you, stop your crying now or I'll give you a reason to cry." She pinched my left arm a little below the shoulder for emphasis. I pulled away from her and pressed myself against the inside of the car door.

We sat in silence. My cheek leaned against the car window. A few remaining tears streaked down the window, pooling onto the rubber seal and making it look shiny. I kept my face away from my mother's view so that she wouldn't know I was disobeying her. We drove past the stores all along Main Street and down the dirt road that was a shortcut to our street. My eyes stayed fixed to my right as we climbed the hill leading to our house, with each of the neighbors' houses lining the right side of the street coming into and then fading from my view. There were no sidewalks on our street. Lawns were separated from the asphalt road only by a three-inch cement curb.

By the time we reached the top of the court, my tears had dried and I turned to see if my mother was still angry. She was concentrating on her driving, looking to make sure that none of the neighborhood kids were playing inside the court. Upon reaching our house, a Swiss chalet that stood at the top of the court's circle, she turned slowly into our driveway. She hit the button of the garage remote control that was clipped to the driver's side visor as she started the steep descent to our basement-level garage. After parking, she fingered the remote again and shut the garage door. Without a word, she handed me the stack of papers she had picked up from the high school. I carried them into the house for her and dropped the quizzes on the kitchen table, then rushed to my bedroom and closed the door behind me.

My mother didn't understand my feelings. It didn't feel right that a boy younger and smaller than I would have the nerve—think he had the right—to bother me just because of the way I looked. I knew my mother wouldn't want to hear about how I dreamed about being more like my white friends in school, how I often stared into the mirror, trying to imagine that I had blue or green eyes and curlier, lighter hair. Or how I wished I were a boy so that I could fight with nasty little boys like that. To my mother, my wishes would just seem foolish and impractical. If I didn't want to receive her scorn, I knew better than to share my thoughts with her.

What's the matter, Sya Meh?

Ah Kung? I thought you were gone.

Don't you remember my promise?

How come you're here for me and not your own daughter?

My daughter is grown and married to a successful man. She doesn't need me. Besides, she always had a bit of her mother in her, occupied with the material. You know, my wife could have lived with me in Shanghai, but she liked it better when I left her alone. That way, she could use the money I sent her any way she liked.

Didn't you ever want to go back to China to see them?

I planned to one time. But before the trip, I got a fortune from the Buddhist temple. Your mother read it to me. It said, "If you take a journey now, it will be very hard. You will have to cross angry oceans and climb steep mountains. And you will never return." So, I stayed with you. Now tell me what's bothering you.

I don't like it when people remind me that I'm different. And I can't even tell Mom about it because I know she'll just get angry at me for feeling that way. What am I supposed to do about it, Ah Kung?

I can't tell you what to do. But maybe I can still help you.

How?

Tell me what you're thinking so it becomes clearer in your own mind. That's how you will know what to do. But remember, you do not know what it's like to be someone else. That's something you should consider before you judge others.

You mean like my mother?

Exactly.

My mother was born in Shanghai and, according to the family legend, is a descendent of an ancient and much honored prime minister of China. The official line of descent, however, didn't pass on to her because the rules of Chinese genealogy only bestow that honor to males. As my mother descended from a female member of the "Zia" clan, she could never claim the Zia name. But the story was passed on to her anyway.

The story of Prime Minister Zia is that of an impoverished scholar. In the legend, it is said that Zia was so poor that, when his wedding party went to pick up the bride that had been promised to him in childhood, his betrothed's family changed its mind. They didn't want their daughter marrying such a poor man. The wedding party was too ashamed to return to Zia empty-handed, so on their way home they stopped at a river where a group of young women were washing clothes. The carriage driver explained that his master, a poor but scholarly young man, was looking for a wife. One of the young peasant women decided that it was a good risk to marry a scholar, even though he was poor. And so, she joined the wedding party to marry young Zia.

Zia was very studious, and his peasant wife took good care of him so he could concentrate on his studies. When it came time to take the national imperial examination, they were both hopeful that he would do well. But poor scholarly Zia exceeded everyone's expectations by getting the highest score of anyone in the country. Under Confucian law, the man who earned that honor became the nation's prime minister. Every several years after that, the national imperial exam was readministered but, because Zia was so brilliant, he remained prime minister for over thirty years.

Zia's peasant wife did not have it so easy. Although she was Zia's number one wife, he was able to take on many concubines after he became prime minister. With his new high status, his concubines came from the most refined families in China. Zia was often invited to bring his wife to have tea at the empress's residence. Each time he would bring one of his sophisticated concubines, and each time the empress would recognize the bound feet of an aristocrat. The empress had heard stories about the big feet of Zia's wife, and so she would chide him, "But this is not your number one wife, is it? I want to meet her." After running through his concubines, Zia finally gave up trying to fool the empress and informed his first peasant wife that she was to meet the empress for tea.

"But what about my big feet?" Zia's wife asked in horror.

"Wear a long dress and don't pass through any doors in her presence, and you will be fine," he assured her. The palace doors had frames that stood a half-foot above the floor. He knew that if she had to go through any doors in front of the empress, his wife's feet would show from beneath her dress. His wife agreed to the plan.

At first the empress didn't know what to make of the long dress worn by Zia's wife. She suspected that Zia had figured out her secret of detecting imposters and was trying to fool her again with another concubine. But she knew she could find the truth soon enough, so she decided to relax and get to know her new guest.

The empress perceived that Zia's wife had a genuine quality about her. She was intelligent, having absorbed a lot of knowledge from when she helped Zia with his studies, and there was beauty beneath her skin that the empress considered missing from the concubines she had met. The empress still wanted to be sure she was meeting the number one wife. When tea was finished, the empress beckoned Zia's wife to join her in the study to see the palace library. Zia's wife was petrified. After having had such a nice time with the empress, she regretted that her big feet would now be revealed and would ruin everything. The empress insisted that they go into the next room. Zia's wife obeyed with a heavy heart and braced for embarrassment.

As Zia's wife crossed the threshold into the study, her big feet were revealed. When the empress saw them, she ran over and gave Zia's wife a big hug. "*You* are the real number one wife," she joyously exclaimed. "I'm so glad to finally meet you."

Zia's wife began to cry from joy, surprised by the empress's reaction. The empress tried to comfort her. "Please don't be mad at me. I just wanted your husband to stop trying to fool me."

"But I'm so ashamed of my big feet," Zia's wife sobbed.

The empress looked at her with kindness. She walked over to the library desk and picked up four solid gold paperweights. She handed them to Zia's wife. "Here, sew these into the hem of your dress and even when you have to pass through doors, your unbound feet can always remain our secret."

What do you think that story tells you about your mother?

That she prefers peasants to aristocrats. And she values compassion.

Anything else?

I guess she wants me to study hard to get ahead.

Yes, that's probably right. But is there more to the story she wants to share?

She wants me to realize that I've had things pretty easy and shouldn't complain all the time.

Compared to what?

To her living through war, I guess.

When the Japanese invaded China, my mother's father took part in a violent demonstration to protest the occupation. My grandfather was put in jail for his part in the protest. While he served his time in Shanghai, my grandmother fled with the children to the safety of Hong Kong. Shortly after arriving there, she gave birth to my mother's little sister—their third child. Disappointingly, the third child was another girl like her two older sisters. My grandparents were separated for six months during the occupation. As the war came to an end, my grandfather summoned my grandmother to join him back in Shanghai. My grandmother's family pleaded for her not to take the baby on the long and treacherous trip, warning that if she took the baby, something terrible would happen. But my grandfather had never even met his youngest child and my grandmother couldn't conceive of leaving the baby behind. Although she made the trip safely, my mother's little sister caught pneumonia shortly after she turned three, and she died. The family blamed the little girl's death on my grandmother for her arrogance and disobedience.

Years later, my mother lived through another war—China's Communist Revolution. In many ways, my mother sympathized with the revolutionaries. She too was bothered by the excesses of the very wealthy and the destitution of the majority, particularly after the war with Japan.

"You know, not everything the communists did was so bad," she once explained. "Before the revolution, many days I would walk to school and hear babies cry. The babies were left in alleys to die because their families couldn't feed them. After the communists took over, I never heard those babies cry anymore. Now, you tell me. What's so wrong with that?"

But while she was studying physics at the University in Shanghai, she realized that the communists were also a force to be feared. Just before her final exams in 1957, students were asked to give up their studies to participate in Mao Tse Tung's latest initiative, the Hundred Flowers Bloom campaign. The campaign, which used the slogan "Let a hundred flowers bloom," was a short-lived crusade to encourage constructive criticism of government. (Government officials later targeted many who criticized the government during the campaign for retribution.) My mother tried to reason with her fellow students to wait until *after* the university exams were over before they became engaged in the campaign. One morning, when she arrived at the gates of the university, she was greeted by a large cartoon sprawled across one of the outside walls of the courtyard, depicting a caricature that looked disturbingly like her. The caption read: "Some people think exams are more important than the future of this country!"

The apparent attack on her was disturbing and when her parents invited her shortly after to join them in Hong Kong, she decided it was a good time to get out of the country. She had a friend, a fellow student, who was a communist party member and was respected for being of the peasant class. It was instinct that made her feel him out first before applying for a travel visa. She explained to her classmate that she was reluctant to see her parents, who were sure to have been corrupted by the capitalist environment of Hong Kong. Her friend listened to her sympathetically. A few weeks later, the friend met her on the street and casually asked why she hadn't yet applied for her visa. She knew then that he had secured an approval for her. What she told her friend helped her leave China, but the feelings she had expressed about her parents and Hong Kong were only partially untrue.

"I hated Hong Kong," she said to me with an expression of tasting something sour. "The people in Hong Kong think they are so much better than real Chinese. But who they really worship are the British. You know, when you went to the movies, they'd play "God Save the Queen" and everyone would jump to their feet. When I got to Hong Kong, I made my parents promise me that if I couldn't get to America, they would let me return to the mainland. If I hadn't gotten into college in America, I would've gone back too. I'd rather have been under the communist Chinese than become a subject of the British."

While in Hong Kong, my mother got into the only American school she applied to, Barnard College in New York City. She had studied English in China but, once she got to the United States, she found that she couldn't understand anything anyone said; the sound of the language was completely different from what she had been taught in the classroom. She decided that the only way she was going to learn the language was to immerse herself in it. She instituted a self-imposed segregation from all other Chinese-speaking students, including her best friend who had gotten into Barnard a year earlier, just so she wouldn't be tempted to speak anything but English.

"I was fluent in English within six months," my mother boasted. Her voice has only the hint of the accent characteristic of most people who immigrated late in their lives. At the end of her period of segregation to learn English, she allowed herself to attend meetings of Columbia University's Chinese Student Union where she met my father. My parents married on the day after my mother's graduation, missing her senior prom (which was still a cherished event in the days my parents went to college).

My mother earned a degree in physics and got a full-time job working for the astronomy lab at Columbia, where she had interned as a student. A little over a year after getting married, she became pregnant with my brother. After Martin was born, she continued working at the university until she was offered a more prestigious job with a large chemical company. At her interview with the chemical company, she was asked if she was planning to get pregnant again. It hadn't even crossed her mind, so she felt honest in answering no. She was plagued with guilt when she found herself pregnant with me only six months into her new job. She was making good money—more than my father was earning from his entry-level position at the Federal Reserve Bank, she likes to remind us—and she enjoyed her work. But a decision had to be made. One of my parents was going to have to stay home now that there were going to be two children to raise. Together my parents reasoned that my father's career in banking had the greater potential for financially supporting the family. Thus, my mother resigned from her position two days before I was born. Physics was a field that would change rapidly after her departure. My mother knew this and left her position knowing that she could never return to it.

Maybe that's why she's always so angry with me. Because I made her sacrifice her career as a physicist.

Ah Sya Meh. Don't act so simple.

Well, it would explain why she gets angry at me all the time.

Perhaps… But what explains why you are always angry with her?

The song rang in my ears: "Chinese, Japanese, dirty knees, what are these?"

CHAPTER 3

What Are You Looking At?

I must have had a strange expression on my face. "What are you looking at?" Emily asked suddenly. Her head was right next to me, behind my left ear.

I thought of Emily as my best friend. We had known each other since the second grade and became good friends when we were in the same homeroom in the third and fourth grades. When I first started going to the school in kindergarten, I was shy and didn't make friends easily. In my first three years of school, the only classmates with whom I became friendly were two girls who, like me, had brothers in the class three years ahead of us. Martin had made friends with their brothers and we three younger sisters often tagged along with them when they played together. But once Emily befriended me in third grade, her popularity started to rub off on me, making it easier for me to make friends.

Emily and I had been separated for the second year in a row for sixth grade homeroom. Chorus practice was one of the few times during the school day when Emily and I could spend time together. We were both sopranos but, being taller than me, Emily stood in the bleacher row behind me, a little to my left so I could see her out of the corner of my eye and we could converse during breaks. We were practicing a song from the Broadway show *Pippin*.

"Rivers may flow where they can ramble. Eagles will roam where they can fly…"

Emily was imitating our music teacher, Mrs. O'Grady, by opening her mouth as wide as she could and alternately arching and scowling her eyebrows with every other word sung. I had to fight hard to keep from laughing when she did that. Chorus practice was enjoyable because of Emily. But that afternoon, in our break between songs when I would usually turn behind me to whisper to Emily, I became distracted. I was staring over at a tall eighth grader with short, dark hair and brilliant blue eyes who sang at the back of the alto section. Like every other girl in our school, the girl who attracted my gaze wore a school uniform. The spring uniforms were sleeveless, collarless one-piece dresses that zipped up in the back and resembled Handi Wipes. The girl I was looking at was wearing one with a medium blue pattern—preferable, I thought, to the ones with canary yellow or pastel pink stripes. Because of the short haircut, she looked a bit like a tomboy, but she was distinctly feminine in her tightly fitting school dress. Her eyes seemed to sparkle, as did the shiny wire retainer that showed each time she smiled. The girl was two years ahead of me and I knew her name from the chorus roll call. She struck me that afternoon as exceptionally attractive.

Emily's question broke me out of my trance.

I was embarrassed to be caught staring at and thinking about the eighth grader. I answered Emily hesitantly in a slow, measured whisper. "I was just looking at that tall girl in the back. She's kind of funny looking or something."

Emily leaned forward to get closer to my left ear. "How do you mean?"

"I don't know. She's kind of cute." Then quickly added, "Like a puppy or dog or something."

Emily laughed. "You think she has a dog face?"

"Yeah," I answered happily. "Let's call her Dog Face."

"Okay," Emily agreed.

Why are you calling that girl Dog Face, Sya Meh? You are not usually a mean girl.

I think if I'm making fun of her it won't seem so strange. I can stare at her and talk about her all I want.

Why do you want to talk about her?

I guess I like the way she looks for some reason.

If you like her looks, why do you want to make fun of her?

It just doesn't seem normal to want to talk about another girl who's older than me and all, unless I'm making fun of her.

Why not normal?

I have weird thoughts about her. Not like how you're supposed to think of other girls. I want to look at her and talk about her, and I don't want my friends thinking I'm weird. It seems easier to make fun of her and call her names than to let anyone know how I really feel.

How do you really feel?

Maybe like Papa felt when he met Mom.

The first time my father saw my mother was at a dance sponsored by the Chinese Student Club of Columbia University. He told me the story of how their romance blossomed one day while we were playing a game of pool downstairs next to Ah Kung's old room. I asked my father between shots how he had gotten my mother to like him. As he recalled how it happened, his face took on the expression of a little boy who had just gotten caught doing something mischievous. He remembered being struck by her immediately.

"I was very cautious when I first met her. I was taken by her looks, of course. But somehow, I realized that she was different from other people that I had dated before. I mean, I was no great ladies' man or anything. I certainly had dates when I was young. But I wasn't a great and experienced, you know uh, 'hunk' by any means. So when I met her, I was very cautious. Instead of just introducing myself as I normally would—'cause I was never shy about any of those things—I would just kind of have the attitude, 'well, there's nothing lost' if I introduced myself or asked someone out. But with your mother I felt I needed a formal introduction. Since it was a Chinese dance, well, the president of the club that year was one of my best friends, so I asked him to introduce us. After he did, I think I had maybe one dance with her, maybe two. And there was no real connection. I called her up a few times after the dance to ask her out, but she kept saying no."

"What did you do?" I asked eagerly.

"Well, I thought if she got used to seeing me she might change her mind. So, I found out from my friend with the Chinese club that Mom took a physics class at Pupin, the science building, three days a week at eight in the morning. I had a class at nine at Hamilton Hall, all the way on the other side of the campus, but every morning as her class was being let out, I would casually walk towards Pupin so I could pass your mother as she left the building. Each morning I would say a casual hi to her and she would smile at me and kind of politely acknowledge me as I walked past her into the building. Sometimes, if I timed it right I could hold the door for her on her way out. She didn't know that I was studying art history and had no reason to be going to the science building. She just assumed that I had a class there that started when hers was ending. But I would simply turn the corner once I got in the building, walk down one of the halls, and wait a few minutes to make sure that she'd be gone and then have to rush all the way across campus to make it to my class, always a few minutes late."

My father was smiling at the recollection and absently took a shot at one of his solid balls, missing the pocket by several inches to the right.

It was my turn at the table, but I wanted to hear more of the story. I had never thought of my father as such a romantic before. My mother had certainly never mentioned it. "How did you finally get Mom to go out with you?"

"Well, I waited 'til it was almost too late. I spent the whole semester passing by her three times a week on her way from her physics class. Near the end of the semester, I tried to make conversation with her—small talk, like the weather or current events. Sometimes I'd try to work in that I was going to be in a track meet for the varsity track team, to try to impress her. But by the end of the fall semester, I hadn't broached the subject of a date again. I knew I couldn't go through another semester of running all around campus just to pretend to bump into her. So, I worked up the nerve to ask her out on the very last day of classes. I was so relieved when she said 'yes' and accepted dinner on a Sunday. It was a good move, because a Sunday dinner out was something she really appreciated because she didn't like the dinners at Barnard on Sundays. They always served a fancy brunch early in the day, so Sunday dinners were just cold leftovers."

I had sunk one of my striped balls as my father spoke. I shot at another one, sinking it in the side pocket. "And Mom liked you right away after that?"

My father laughed. "No, I had competition then. Your mother was also being courted by the son of a big-time rich businessman from Hong Kong. I was still in school and my family no longer had money. I worried that I couldn't compete that way. I once took her to a football game and that was kind of a disaster. I remember someone spilling beer on me and she wasn't very impressed with me. But I think what finally won her over was when I took her to the art museum. Because your mother, you know, naturally has this great love of learning. And when I took her to the museum something changed for her. She seemed to enjoy being with me because I could tell her so much about the paintings we saw. And that was probably the connection that led to our getting married."

I was well ahead in the game by then. I hadn't won yet, but my father was too distracted and put down his stick, concentrating on the story. I prompted him to finish the story and we forgot about the rest of the game.

My father said he proposed to my mother at Tom's Restaurant, an inexpensive diner that was a popular hangout for Columbia students. I later tried to confirm my father's recollection with my mother, but she claimed not to recall how or where Papa proposed. She didn't dispute it; she said she just couldn't remember. My mother did remember that she had received a fortune cookie at the end of one of her dates with my father. Supposedly it said: "You will receive two proposals. The darker one loves you more." My father tans very easily. But my mother said that the fortune wasn't the reason she chose to marry my father over the Hong Kong businessman who had, as the fortune predicted, also proposed to her. But it probably didn't hurt.

Like my mother, my father was born in Shanghai, China, in 1938. He was the baby of six siblings. My father's mother was a native of Shanghai. My paternal grandfather had Chinese parents but was born in Hawaii, then a territory of the United States. He was said to have been one of the earliest ethnically Chinese graduates of Harvard University, and he arranged for the donation of his class's gift to Harvard—a huge statue of a tortoise right in the middle of Harvard Yard. While at Harvard, my grandfather befriended fellow student T.V. Soong, future brother-in-law of and finance minister for Chiang Kai-shek. Soong convinced my grandfather to repatriate to China after graduation, and ultimately to serve in the Kuomingtang (Nationalist Party) government as customs general. The post reportedly made my grandfather one of the highest-ranking officials in China. It was also boasted that my grandfather acted as escort and protector to one of Soong's sisters while she attended Wellesley College—before she became Madame Chiang Kai-shek.

Over the years, I learned in bits and pieces (mostly from my father's siblings) that my grandfather had remained in China throughout World War II and resisted the Japanese during the invasion and occupation of China. When all the highest-level Kuomingtang officials got threats that their families would be kidnapped by Japanese invaders if they didn't cooperate, he sent his young family to Hawaii for safety but remained in China himself, continuing to defy Japanese authority. After Pearl Harbor, the family moved from Hawaii to California. But my grandfather did not join them until 1946 when the war was over, and it became clear that Mao Tse-tung's communists were coming to power.

At age eight, meeting his own father for the first time, my father had trouble relating the real-life man introduced as his father with the man he had heard so many stories about. My father explained, "There was some disappointment when my father first came to California because he had been kind of blown out of proportion in the stories I had heard growing up. For example, I imagined him to be a large and powerful man. But when he joined us, he turned out to be only about five feet, four inches tall. And he was already quite elderly. When I was young, I would ask him to play ball with me, as he had bragged that he used to play baseball. But he always refused. I never really got to know him as a teenager either. I would try to discuss politics with him because by then I was becoming more knowledgeable about China and history. I felt that the Kuomingtang government did not live up to its responsibilities in leading the country. So, I used to challenge my father about his interpretation of history in the Chiang Kai-Shek years. But he always acted aloof and distant to me."

The man I knew as "Yeh Yeh," "paternal grandfather" in the Shanghai dialect, was far from the important and powerful man he might have once been. The last time we had my Yeh Yeh over for dinner, he sat stiffly and proudly at the head of the dining room table. He always wore a suit and tie when he visited from his Yonkers nursing home. He complimented my mother on the chicken, which he dipped in oyster sauce that came in a bottle like ketchup. When my mother modestly explained that she had simply boiled the chicken, he boasted, "Yes, but nobody boils chicken like the Chinese." After chewing on a bite and swallowing it, he laid down his chopsticks in a deliberate motion and focused his gaze at my brother and me. Martin and I were seated next to each other near the foot of the table. "What grades do you each attend?" my grandfather asked.

"I'm in fifth," I answered.

"And I'm in eighth," Martin offered.

"And do you have a favorite subject?" Yeh Yeh inquired.

"I like social studies," I told him.

"And why is that?"

"We learned about archeology and stuff. You know, digging up things thousands of years old. It's pretty cool."

"Wonderful. And you?" he asked my brother. "Do you have a favorite subject?"

"English."

"From a standpoint of literature or composition?"

"Both, I guess," Martin responded.

"That's just fine. I'm so pleased to hear it."

Sitting on either side of my grandfather, my parents looked at each other with stunned smiles. My parents had explained to us a year earlier that Yeh Yeh suffered from senility and his lucidity that night seemed a pleasant surprise.

Then my grandfather leaned forward, with a concentrated expression. His scrunched-up face and the way he held his head, kind of bent down and forward, reminded me of a cartoon character: either some turtle or maybe a book worm with glasses that made his eyes bulge. "And tell me. Who are your parents?"

Martin and I fought to keep from laughing. We looked at my father, whose expression now looked sad. "They are my children," my father explained.

"Of course. And you attended Harvard with me, yes?" Yeh Yeh said. My father didn't bother correcting him that evening, and it was the last time we had Yeh Yeh over for dinner. He died shortly after at the age of 89.

The only story that stuck in my mind about my father's mother, whom we called "Un Nah," Shanghai dialect for "paternal grandmother," was about when her father died. It was said that she had a vision one night that her father came to her from across the sea and sat at the edge of her bed to say goodbye. In the morning, she wore a red barrette in her hair. When her husband asked about the barrette, she told him that she was mourning for her father, who she believed had died the night before. Just at that moment, according to the story, the phone rang. It was a call from China, informing her that her father had in fact died that night.

Uh Nah died when I was only six, so I never really got to know her. I remembered visiting the hospital where she was dying of cancer.

Martin and I were considered too young to go up to the patient floors. So, my mother convinced us that, if we waved to the security camera in the downstairs lobby, my grandmother would be able to see us. My memories of Un Nah came vaguely from my memory and from pictures my father kept of her. She had an oval face, with prominent cheekbones, thick lips, and a bright smile. Her greying hair was always pulled back from her face and neatly arranged in a bun at the crown of her head. She played cards with my brother, but I never had a chance to do much with her. For me, she wasn't much more than a pleasant and benevolent memory.

Yet my father thought of his mother as an exceptionally strong and supportive person. Before arriving in this country, as a member of the gentry and ruling class, she never had to know how to cook or drive or do any housework. Ah Kung had been secured as her servant when both of them were teenagers. But all that changed when she moved to America, originally without her husband. My father speaks of it proudly. "Growing up, while maybe she had a little bit of a hard time keeping up with all the housework with six children at home, your Un Nah did just about everything else for us. And when times got tough, she took in work stringing beads, even when her eyesight was going. But she was still a proud woman. When she found out that I was going around the neighborhood when I was six or seven charging people fifty cents to sharpen their knives on a sandstone—which was an outrageous amount at the time, but I guess my customers thought I was cute—she was embarrassed by it and made me stop. Un Nah was a pretty remarkable woman."

Uh Nah and Yeh Yeh both lost a lot by moving to America. They had to give up money, power, prestige, and servants. I guess they didn't have a choice, but, I bet if they did, they would have wanted to keep their lives on easy street.

Those things you speak of don't bring happiness. The Buddha teaches that the origin of suffering is clinging to and craving those things. If their lives here helped them abandon their desire for them, it put them on a far better path than "easy street."

I don't get it. Why would anyone not want things to be easier?

Perhaps to grow and learn.

My father's earliest years in America were spent in Claremont, California, east of Los Angeles. He learned to speak English easily as a two-year-old immigrant and retained little of the Shanghai and Mandarin dialects spoken by his parents. He had American friends and always got along with his peers. Before he started high school, his family moved to the East Coast to Yonkers, New York. As a youth, my father was more concerned about sports (he played football, baseball, soccer, and competed in several events in track and field) than about schoolwork. According to my Auntie Zoe, my father couldn't read until he was in sixth grade because she used to love to read to him, as the baby of the family, and do his homework for him. She finally stopped coddling him and forced him to learn to read when she realized he was largely illiterate at the age of eleven. While attending public high school, he read the Classic Comics versions of *Moby Dick* and other reading assignments rather than the actual books. In his freshman year at his Yonkers high school he was voted Most Popular in his class and was the first freshman to get pledged to his high school fraternity, one of four that ran the school in terms of athletics and social activities. In his sophomore year, he was voted to the student council. But academically he was on the road to being the family delinquent in comparison to his older siblings, who had all received scholarships to attend prestigious colleges. Before his junior year he suddenly realized that he needed to do something to secure his own future.

Hotchkiss was one of a handful of celebrated New England boarding schools. My father crammed for an entrance exam and wrote an essay application to that institution, still relying to an extent on some of the shortcuts (Classic Comics and crib notes) that got him passing grades in public school. Miraculously (his description), he earned a full scholarship to attend Hotchkiss for his last two years of high school. He recalls the academic challenges he faced coming in as a junior. He also recalled a particular incident in a math class.

"My teacher was fond of using the phrase, 'If you don't study hard, you don't have a Chinaman's chance of passing.' He said it several times over the semester and used it again before the midterm exam. But then he must have suddenly realized that I was in his class and added, 'But I should say that no Chinese person has ever failed one of my exams.' Of course, I managed to fail that exam. But it made me work harder the rest of the semester so I was able to pass the course in the end."

From Hotchkiss, he was able to obtain a scholarship to attend Columbia College where he met my mother.

I sure hope someday I'll meet someone like Papa did.

Someone like the girl you call Dog Face?

A girl? How could that be?

You made the comparison, Sya Meh.

In the end, making fun of and calling the girl Dog Face backfired. She discovered that Emily and I were making fun of her and one day cornered Emily to demand to know why we were doing it. Emily innocently asked her, "Would you rather us call you 'Puppy Face?'"

The girl became so enraged that she actually slapped Emily hard across the face.

Feeling guilty about having instigated the whole thing, I invited Emily over to my house and we called the girl to apologize and promised never to make fun of her again. Reluctantly the girl accepted our apology. But after that, the girl never wanted to have anything to do with me.

It doesn't look like I'm going to get to be like Papa that way.

No. Not that way.

PART 2

American Me

CHAPTER 4
Nobody Invited You

Adam and I ducked out from the lobby of the ski hostel while the chaperones and all the other students were warming their feet around a large hearth. Quietly, we tiptoed up the south stairs to the boys' side of the hostel. Like the girls' side, each room was furnished with two bunk beds. Adam jumped up onto one of the top bunks in his room. He reached his hand down to pull me up.

I was happy as a sophomore in high school. Although Emily had abandoned me in the eighth grade to go to the town's public school, we were still friends and I built on the popularity that my friendship with her had given me. I was now one of the "in" crowd—one of the few of my classmates that had been at the school since kindergarten—and had accumulated of a lot of friends over the years. I was part of the clique that got to decide whether or not a new student would be accepted as part of the circle that gave and went to all the important parties, or if he or she would be relegated to a less popular group of friends. I enjoyed the power my status gave me. But there was still one aspect of popularity that I hadn't mastered: dating.

Adam was one of the best-looking boys in our class, with chiseled, dark features and beautiful, curly black hair. He had been dating a girl named Carrie but on the bus ride up to Stowe, he told me that he and Carrie were history.

Staring down at me anxiously, smiling with his perfect white teeth, he pleaded, "Come on up. It's all right, nobody will walk in on us."

I took his hand and let him help me up to his bunk. He kissed me and quickly and expertly unhooked my bra. But I refused to take my shirt off. He pushed me back on top of the sheets and reached under my shirt to feel me up. On his knees, he straddled me, and while still kissing me, he unzipped his pants and pulled them down. I felt him poking at me through his underwear.

"Hey, Adam. That's as far as I want to go now, okay?"

"Okay," he groaned. "But you don't really know what you're missing."

"I'll take your word for it."

We kissed some more in that position on the bed. I left his room and snuck back to mine before the chaperones noticed we were missing.

>*What a stupid girl!*
>
>*Are you saying something to me, Ah Kung?*
>
>>*I was talking to myself, Sya Meh. But since you overheard me, maybe you have something to say about it.*
>
>*I'm not stupid. Everyone does it. If anything, I've held off a lot longer than my friends.*
>
>>*Letting that boy do such things shows no respect for yourself.*
>
>*It had to happen sometime.*
>
>>*Do you even like that boy?*
>
>*Well he is awfully conceited. But he's also very good-looking.*
>
>>*How trivial!*

When the ski trip was over, Adam and Carrie got back together as a couple. On the bus ride back home, Carrie's friends told her about how Adam and I had made out. I tried to let her know through some of our mutual friends that Adam had sworn to me that they had broken up. But the message that got back to me was that she didn't care what Adam told me. I should have known better and stayed away from him.

Carrie made it her mission that year to make my life hell. She was a member of the cheerleading squad and could count on most of her fellow cheerleaders to treat me with the same contempt she did. That year, one of her cheerleader friends was the host of the *Fiddler on the Roof* cast party for that year's school play. I was a member of the crew that constructed the sets, and the boy I was dating was one of the play's six major stars—the only sophomore to have secured a role with a solo performance. Naturally, I expected to go to the party. As I approached the door of the home where the party was being held, I was already a little drunk from indulging earlier with some of my friends who were also involved with the play.

"Nobody invited you," the host told me, holding her arm across the screen door so I couldn't enter.

"What do you mean? I'm on the crew. My boyfriend Josh played Perchik."

"So what. After what you did to Carrie, you're not welcome." The cheerleader slammed the door in my face.

Banishment from the big party in my state of inebriation was a heavy blow. I couldn't stop crying, even when Josh came out of the party to try to comfort me. I think I would have cried in a drunken stupor outside all night if the neighbor with whom I carpooled to school all year hadn't felt sorry for me and agreed to leave the party early and take me home. I was grateful that, as a senior and captain of the cheerleading squad, my neighbor wouldn't take her marching orders from a sophomore on her team.

Thankfully, Carrie's vengeance against me only lasted a short time past the cast party. By the end of the year, Carrie and Adam broke up for good. He started dating an older girl that he met at a club in New York City and Carrie hooked up with an upperclassman.

I never ever want to go through anything like that again. That was the worst experience of my life.

Then you're a very lucky girl.

Maybe you don't know what it's like when people you thought were your friends suddenly hate you. I've really worked hard to be part of the popular crowd. And that wasn't easy, being Chinese and all. I think of it as a pretty big accomplishment. Think about those two friends that I used to hang out with because their brothers were friends with Martin. They never got to be popular. They're both considered nerds and I barely even say hi to them anymore.

Is that something to be proud of, Sya Meh?

Yes, I am proud of being popular. Absolutely. I think I just can't go out with boys that any of the girls in my class have dated or want to date.

Over the summer between my sophomore and junior years, I got involved with Peter. He was the twenty-four-year-old brother of Joni, my classmate and close friend. I had met Peter a few times when I was over at Joni's house and had even slow danced with him at her Sweet Sixteen birthday party. He was handsome and seemed worldly to me, with his moustache and his nine years on me (I had a late birthday so I was still only fifteen). Peter was playing tennis with a friend one summer evening at the same time and at the same indoor courts where my father and I always played. He recognized me right away and acted friendly in an older brother kind of way, and was polite and respectful to my father. He complimented me on my tennis game and suggested in front of my father that we get together and play some evening. I was excited about the thought of spending an evening with him, even if it was just to play tennis. Peter said he'd get my number from Joni and give me a call to set it up.

He called less than a week later and asked if I had a regular court at the club. I did. My father let me use the court with Peter that week. Peter picked me up twenty minutes before eight in his black Toyota hatchback with a red racing stripe—a car that came from the dealership his father owned and where Peter worked as a salesman. The two of us played tennis for an hour at the indoor courts. I was a better tennis player, but I made sure that he kept even with me. When the buzzer rang, sounding the end of the hour, our score was tied up at six-all in games.

It was dark already when we stepped outside to get to his car, and the cool breeze gave me a chill since I was still damp from sweating. I moved quickly to the car so I could get inside and be protected from the night air. We both jumped into the car and quickly shut the doors. But Peter didn't start the car right away.

He turned to me and leaned closer to me, with his right hand on the back of my seat. "You don't know how glad I was to run into you at the tennis courts last week. I thought about you a lot after dancing with you at Joni's party."

"Really?" I was still a little bit out of breath.

"Really." He leaned even closer and kissed me. Then pulled back a bit. "You haven't had much experience kissing, have you?"

"What do you mean?" I asked. I was insulted by his question.

"Well, you keep your lips kind of tight."

"I just wasn't expecting you to kiss me right here, right after tennis. Try it again."

He did. "No, it's not that," he said. "Why don't you let me teach you? I can teach you a lot of things, you know."

"I don't need you to teach me anything."

His voice softened. "I don't mean it that way. But I think I can help you enjoy kissing more. Will you let me try?"

"What do I have to do?"

"Relax your lips a little. And let them part."

We tried again.

"Yeah," he said. "That's much better."

He taught me a few other things that evening before dropping me back home. I told my parents that we had gone out for a milkshake after playing.

I'm worried about you, Sya Meh.

Why? I'm just doing what normal fifteen-year-old girls are supposed to do.

How do you know that is what other girls your age do?

My closest friends don't really talk about it a whole lot. But a lot of them have had serious boyfriends. I'm sure they've all done things at least close to what Peter and I did. And Adam obviously wanted to go all the way with me right away. So if he went out with Carrie all that time, they must have gone pretty far, if not the whole way.

Will you see Peter again?

I hope so.

And if he wants to take it further? He's much older than you. Don't you think he'll expect more from you?

What's the big deal anyway? As long as I don't get pregnant or anything, and there are ways to get around that. Besides, I don't even know if or when I'll see him again. Maybe it was just this one-time thing. He wanted to teach poor little inexperienced me some things about the art of love.

I think you will hear from him again.

Yeah, that's what I think too.

Peter called two days later and told me to tell my parents that he wanted to take me out to dinner to pay me back for letting him use our court time. He told them that we were going to a restaurant famous for its hamburgers over in the next town. We did go to the restaurant, but he just picked up the food to go. Then we went back to his apartment. We ate dinner and then we had sex. I was just finishing my period and I don't even think I bled. In all, I thought it was okay, but there was really no big deal to it.

Peter called the next day to see how I was and to see if I would think about spending a weekend at Joni's while his parents were out of town, so he could come over and we could see each other again. I told him I didn't really want to go out with him. I think it hurt his ego to have a fifteen-year-old break up with him.

Was it what you expected?

Hardly even worth talking about. I don't suppose sex was ever very important to you.

I did my duty as a husband. But, no. It was never something that occupied much of my attention. Would it be different if you cared for him more?

Maybe. But I don't really get all that excited about guys. At least not in an emotional way. I guess maybe dating just isn't my thing. I like it as much, if not better, to just hang out with my friends as a group. Besides, I have more important things to worry about.

Like what?

Well, I almost failed chemistry last year. If I don't do a lot better in physics I might not get into a good college.

My junior year physics class was filled with some of my best friends. Two of my best girlfriends, Sarah and Carol; Emmet, the class clown (but also really smart); and my closest friend, a boy named Kendall, had all signed up for the class. The teacher, Mr. Norman, came from teaching at a public school down in Trenton. He told us that on the first day of class and also told us he expected us to be better students than the ones he taught in Trenton. The things we learned that year were much more interesting and easier for me to understand than chemistry. I got a taste of why my Mom had liked physics. But mostly, the class was just a lot of fun because I got to work on interesting experiments and projects with my friends.

Mr. Norman never collected the homework assignments, so I stopped doing them. I figured out how to count, from where I sat, which homework question he would ask me to solve and I would quickly work out the answer before he called on me. That way I could get away with only doing one out of maybe twenty-five questions each day. We had two exams in the course, a midterm and final, both of which took a full class period. But Mr. Norman was a strange teacher: after he passed out the tests, he turned towards the blackboard and buried his head in a book with his back to us. Through both exams, not once did he turn around to look at the students taking the test. When any one of us got stuck on a problem, we could get up very quietly and look over at another student's work and figure out how to solve it. My friends and I were jumping all over the room to make sure we got all the answers right. He never turned around to catch us cheating and all my friends and I got A's in physics that year.

Mr. Norman must be so grateful to not have to teach in Trenton anymore that he didn't care what we did. He must have known we were cheating, even with his back to us.

You think it meant he didn't care?

If he cared—if he had been more attentive to us while we were taking the tests—none of us would have dared to cheat.

Maybe he was trying to teach you all something else beyond physics.

I'm not sure what you mean, Ah Kung.

What did you learn?

A little about physics. But I didn't need to learn that much in order to get an A this year.

And that hurts him in what way?

I don't know that it hurts him.

What about you?

You don't have to ruin it for me. An A is an A. It really doesn't matter how you get it.

If you say so.

That's right. And right now, I just want to get through school and have a little fun with my friends before we all have to separate when we go to college.

You're very loyal to your friends, aren't you?

Sure I am.

Even if they aren't always loyal to each other?

On the alcove wall, just above the steps leading to the math department, the symbol for "null set" scrawled in graffiti caught my attention. It was a zero with a broad line running diagonally through it—a mathematical symbol we had spent a week on in advanced algebra. A couple of my classmates giggled, pointing to the symbol as they passed me on their way up the stairs. The null set graffiti was showing up all through the corridors of the high school. Those of us in the know understood its meaning.

Jen was one of my classmates in the popular crowd. When she caught mononucleosis in junior year, she expected it to be considered a badge of honor, like it had been for the half dozen other students in our clique who had gotten the illness before her. But during Jen's month-long absence, some of our friends used the opportunity to compare complaints they had about her. Before she was deemed noninfectious and able to return to school, there was a virtual consensus among the clique that nobody really liked Jen after all. Her boyfriend started dating a prettier and more popular girl. It was his idea to start the null set campaign to humiliate Jen. The symbol, he explained to everyone, should show Jen now what her "set" of friends looked like: empty.

When I saw the null set sign above the steps, the boldest one yet, I felt sorry for Jen. She was never one of my closest friends, but we had socialized with the same people since the eighth grade. What was happening to Jen reminded me of one of my deepest fears: that I too might one day be exposed as someone who did not truly belong. This terror stirred feelings of compassion that afternoon.

Valentine's Day was just around the corner, and I knew it would be tough on Jen. The school's cheerleaders were selling carnations for the occasion—red ones for people you loved, pink ones for those you secretly admired, and white ones for friends. I purchased a single white carnation and asked the cheerleader I bought it from to wait for me to get a card to be included with the delivery. In secret, I went to as many people as I could get to listen and asked them to sign a card for Jen to help stop the vicious crusade against her. I even got my old friend Emily to sign the card, since she knew Jen when she had gone to private school with us. But most of those who signed the card were other students in the class who were also excluded from the popular crowd—about twenty in all. When the white carnation was delivered to Jen, it was accompanied by the card with the signatures of my recruits, enclosed by a large set of brackets. On the top of the card, I wrote, "Dear Jen, Happy Valentine's Day! From your 'set' of friends." Before the year was over, the tormenters lost interest in their null set campaign and Jen was welcomed back to associate with the popular students.

I'm proud of what you did there, Sya Meh.

It wasn't bad.

It seems you learned something from when people were mean to you.

It would have meant everything for me to have had more people stick up for me like that. Just having my neighbor drive me home from the cast party meant a lot.

So you wanted to do something similar?

More than that. Because I think Jen's ordeal must have been even harder for her than mine, which was bad enough. But at least with me I was only really isolated from the cheerleading squad, while the rest of my friends stuck by me. But it was Jen's closest friends who actually turned on her.

Well, it was a good deed. I'm proud of you.

I was kind of scared doing it, you know, Ah Kung.

Why scared?

It could have made things worse for me. I try most of the time to make people forget that I'm different. So going against everyone in my crowd was a real risk.

Why do you still worry so much about that?

I just want to fit in. There's no real mystery to it.

> *But why always so embarrassed about being different? You're even ashamed of your own grandparents.*

I just don't know why my mother's parents have to live with us now.

> *Why shouldn't they live with you? They moved all the way from Hong Kong to be closer to their children and grandchildren. That should be a blessing to you.*

But I'm just trying to be a normal teenager! Do you know how embarrassing it is to have Gnah Boo answer the phone? She answers it by screaming "Weh?" in that loud Chinese voice of hers. It probably scares my friends half to death when they call.

> *Such worries you have.*

You're telling me.

> *In any case, your kindness to Jen was impressive, despite your concerns. Since someone showed kindness to you when you were troubled, you decided to pass it on to someone else.*

Yeah, and maybe Jen will pass it on too.

My sense of self-satisfaction about my altruistic effort with Jen was destroyed within the first few months of senior year. We were on a class trip to Washington, DC. I happened to get assigned to share a room with my friend Carol, Jen, and another girl named Kelly. Being roommates, we all hung out together. Kelly was one of the quieter girls from the class because she was taller than most of the boys and perhaps a little awkward. But she was kind and gentle and liked by most of her classmates. On the last evening of the excursion, we were taken to a dinner theater presentation of the musical *Gypsy*. I was sitting at a table next to Kelly, and Jen was sitting across from us. I was watching the show when suddenly I heard Jen raise her voice and shout to Kelly, "Don't you know that we don't like you hanging around us all the time? Don't you know that everyone thinks you're a lesbian?" Kelly was surprised by the outburst and began to cry.

I couldn't believe it. Why would Jen, someone who knew firsthand how painful it is to be unjustly attacked by others, turn around and so cruelly make someone else feel that way? I even reminded Jen that *she* of all people should know better. But Jen just picked up the sour cream for her baked potato and threw it onto Kelly's shirt, then stormed away from the table.

I tried to comfort Kelly: "You know nobody else feels that way, don't you? I think Jen's just trying to get back at someone for what happened to her last year."

My words seemed to make Kelly feel a little better. She stopped crying and finished her dinner without further incident.

I should have just let Jen keep suffering last year for all the good it did. The only thing she got out of her experience was the desire to inflict the same kind of pain she went through onto someone else.

    If you feel that way, why did you comfort Kelly? The effort could have been just as wasted on her.

You're right Ah Kung. Maybe I should have learned my lesson.

    But you did it anyway. Why?

I guess I'm still hoping that it'll make a difference for Kelly. Then I'll know I did the right thing.

    Are you saying it was wrong to help Jen since she was mean to Kelly?

I guess so.

But then how can you ever know what is right to do, unless you can see into the future how it will work out?

You're confusing me, Ah Kung.

Choices are in the present, but their results are in the future. If you feel you have to rely on results to make a decision, you may never know how to act.

What else should I use to decide things?

Why did you want to be nice to Jen and then again to Kelly?

Because I was grateful when someone was nice to me.

And do you think your actions were right one time and the other time wrong?

I guess deep down I feel that both times I did the right thing.

So what does that tell you?

You mean if something is the right thing to do, it doesn't matter what happens as a result?

That's right, Sya Meh.

Are you talking about right in God's eyes? 'Cause I'm still not so clear about all that stuff.

Not necessarily.

Then what, Ah Kung?

Think about it.

You mean in my own eyes?

CHAPTER 5

NYC, JUST LIKE
I PICTURED IT

It was unusual for me to want to follow in my mother's footsteps in anything. Thus, it was a surprise to everyone when I decided to go to Barnard. I figured I got into the school because my parents were both alumni of Columbia University. It wasn't my first choice—I was hoping to get into Brown. Brown was the school that the greatest number of my classmates applied to that year, probably because John F. Kennedy Jr. went there. Emily got accepted to Brown, but I got rejected. My guidance counselor and an SAT instructor had advised me that it would be to my benefit to indicate an interest in a more unique prospective major and to emphasize my cultural/ethnic heritage. They explained that you have to be more exceptional to stand out among the thousands of proposed English and psychology majors. I would have an easier time declaring a more obscure area of interest. They also suggested that playing up my cultural background would help with affirmative action programs and give me some latitude for not getting the highest of scores on the English section of my aptitude test. In accordance with their advice, my college applications stated that I was interested in studying anthropology and archaeology with an eye towards fieldwork in China. My essay was written as an imagined dialogue with Lao Tzu, the fifth century BC founder of Taoism. Barnard was the best of the three schools that accepted my application.

College was going to be a whole new life for me. From kindergarten to twelfth grade, I had gone only to one school, a fact that made the prospect of meeting new people and having to make all new friends daunting. Most of my other high school classmates had at least one friend going to the same school or one in close proximity. There was one girl from my high school who was also going to attend Barnard, but she was friends with a different crowd and I always thought of her as kind of a bookworm. I knew I wasn't going to be hanging out with her at college. I also felt strange about going to an all women's college. I told my friends that I was nervous about meeting a bunch of lesbians. But the school was in New York City, and I was excited about the prospect of finally living right in the city rather than in the New Jersey suburbs. I signed up to live off campus in an apartment building owned by the college on West 116th Street, just across the street from campus. I was to share the apartment with three other girls, two to a bedroom.

My parents drove me to school and helped me bring my stuff to the second-floor apartment I was assigned to. I missed most of the orientation activities, however, because I had gotten a job for the second year in a row working as a ball girl at the US Open Tennis Championships. I just had time to drop off my things, introduce myself to my two suitemates (my roommate hadn't yet arrived), and change into my ball girl uniform. Then I had to hop on the subway to get to the tennis center at Flushing Meadows Park in Queens. It was a bit awkward trying to make new friends the first week while I spent most of my time chasing balls at the National Tennis Center. I didn't even get to meet my roommate, Carol, until two days after moving in. She happened to be one of the people I had met briefly a year earlier when we both spent a weekend for prospective students visiting the campus.

I was one of the better ball girls so I got to work a lot of choice matches, mostly in the Louis Armstrong Stadium at night. I would get back to the apartment late almost every day during my first week. I even worked the last weekend of the tournament, including the women's finals. Martina Navratilova won that year and I got to carry her racquets off the court for her while her hands were full with flowers. One of ball boys I was friendly with told me that Martina invited him to her victory party at her hotel and wanted him to invite me and the other girl that worked the match. But I was too scared to go. There was something about Martina (or maybe it was about me) that made me nervous. I went back to my dorm room and kept the activities about the tournament to myself. I started the year feeling very out of place.

> *New surroundings can be hard, Sya Meh. After I came from China, I had to learn to live with another family in a new country. I didn't speak the language or know my surroundings. Do you think it was easy for me?*
>
> *It's just weird being stuck here like this. I don't think I'd naturally become friends with any of my suitemates if we hadn't just happened to be stuck together.*
>
> *Sometimes you must learn to adjust.*
>
> *I always dreamed about living in the city, but I don't even really know how to get around. I know how to get out to the tennis center, but that's about it.*
>
> *When I had to learn how to get around New York by myself, I rode the subway from one end to the other, north to south, east to west. I couldn't read the names of the subway stops, but I could match the letters to the names on the map. It only took me one day of riding to learn. Your mother said I had more sense than your grandfather who went to Harvard. He never mastered riding the subway. For you, it should be easy.*

I can read maps maybe, but not people. And everyone here is so different from me.

Shouldn't this time be about meeting new people?

I'm just not used to being around people so different from me. I can only hope things'll get better once I have a chance to find my kind of person here at Barnard.

What kind is that?

I guess I'll know when I find them.

Victoria, who shared the other bedroom in our apartment, was relatively skilled at meeting people, although she mainly limited herself to befriending other African-American students. Carol didn't seem to care much about making friends. She said she was hoping to transfer to Yale as soon as she could. But Victoria's roommate, Melanie, was a pro at making new friends, certainly the best of the four of us. She got a new boyfriend immediately, someone she met during orientation. He was a year ahead of us and bragged about being an artist. Melanie also made friends with all the Japanese freshman, since she'd been an exchange student in Japan in high school and could speak Japanese. But mostly, she seemed to be drawn to anyone who looked different or unique in some way, and she had a knack for making friends with them. Most of the people I got to know in the first several months of college were people I met through Melanie.

Everyone was so different from my preppy, upper-middle-class friends from high school. I became friends with an adorable little blond girl named Diana who dyed a pink streak in her hair and wore black leather pants. We hung out with Jamie and Alana, a pair of roommates from the campus dorm who buzzed their hair short and used gel to make it stand straight up. Jamie and Alana wore a lot of black leather too, listened to Velvet Underground, and experimented with drugs. Melanie also introduced us all to Jose, a mathematically gifted Puerto Rican scholarship student from Queens who played in a hardcore band and started off the year with a mohawk but later shaved his head completely. Jose got at least four of our little group of friends into bed, including me. In my freshman year, all the girls I socialized with had a lot of experience with sex, except for Carol, who (somewhat to her embarrassment) was still a virgin, and me, who had only had two other sexual encounters after Peter by the time I got to college. My new friends had a very casual attitude toward sex, and the free atmosphere of a New York City college seemed to promote a lot of it.

For a short time, I dated a senior from one of the fraternities. We really didn't have much in common, so I broke up with him a few days after we finally slept together. I thought I might be interested in a good-looking blond guy from my computer class that always sat with me, a girl I knew from my off-campus apartment building, and another good-looking guy from Denmark. The guy from Denmark and the girl from my building got together. But it turned out that the other guy was gay and had really been interested in the Danish boy. At one time, my friend Emmet from high school dropped by while he was visiting his brother, who was a senior at Columbia. We tried to have sex. To Emmet's humiliation though, he had done too much cocaine that night and couldn't really perform. There was also my conquest by Jose, and I went home with a bar manager from a local hangout. But I still really couldn't get serious with any guy I met.

Despite the fear I had expressed to my high school friends, I hadn't met any lesbians at Barnard, either. Yet before long, I found myself hoping that a particular girl was one. I saw her on one of the first days of classes in the bathroom of Milbank Hall. When I walked into the bathroom, she was doing a deep hamstring stretch across the floor. She didn't even look up when I walked around her to get to the stall. But I couldn't take my eyes off her. I could tell right away that she was a dancer. Her body was thin, flat chested, and tall. She had light brown hair, cut very short like a boy's. Her eyes were a color of amber I had never seen before on anyone. When I saw her for the first time, I felt like I couldn't breathe.

Do you want to get to know her?

What would I say? I'd feel like a total idiot trying to meet her out of the blue.

Your friend Melanie has no trouble introducing herself to people she wants to meet. Why should it be hard for you?

It's not something I feel comfortable doing. Unless there's some situation or reason to talk to someone, like to ask them a question in class or something, I can't just strike up a conversation with a total stranger. At parties even, the only way I can manage to do the mingling thing is to be loose with alcohol. It's really much easier for me to make friends with people if someone else introduces them to me. Or if they start talking to me first.

Why leave it up to the other people? Your father didn't.

I'm just not like that.

I tried to find out as much as possible about the girl. She didn't seem new to the school when I first saw her during the first week of classes, so I guessed that she was at least one class ahead of me. I was right about her being a dancer (I saw her at a dance performance held in the school gym one evening) and she seemed to be mostly friendly with other dancers or stage performers. I knew that I was not the only one who noticed her looks. Even Carol and Melanie noticed her, and before any of us knew her name, the three of us would refer to her as "that neat-looking girl" if we saw her at a party. We even had a debate about whether or not we thought she was a lesbian. Carol thought she was, but I wasn't sure. Eventually I learned her name.

Each time I got ready to go to the cafeteria for lunch or dinner (I almost always skipped breakfast), I would get this excited feeling, hoping that I would get a chance to see Harper. I would watch her from across the cafeteria but never approached her. As the end of the first semester was drawing close, I still hadn't spoken a word to her. Then, right in the middle of final exams, I walked into the cafeteria and saw Harper sitting at a table with my friend Diana. My heart felt like it was pounding too fast and I could feel it in my throat. I was battling a cold and I thought I might be getting a fever too because my face felt flush. Diana waved me over to join them. I said hi to Diana and put my jacket down on the seat across from the two of them and walked over to the salad bar to get food. Harper got up when I walked away from the table and I was sad because I thought she was leaving. Disappointed, I returned to the table and started talking with Diana. Then Harper came back with more tuna fish and bread and sat back down with us.

"So how was the movie last night?" Diana asked me.

"Pretty good, but weird." I answered.

"Oh, what movie was it?" Harper asked. It was the first time she ever addressed me.

"*Nosfaratu*," I answered in a voice that I thought sounded annoyed. I wanted to say more to her but my mind was blank. Diana talked to me awhile about our psychology final coming up. I forced myself not to stare at Harper.

As Diana and I were discussing psychology, Harper leaned over toward my lunch tray, noticing that I also had gotten tuna fish. "Does this tuna taste right to you?" she asked.

"I don't know. I have a cold and can't taste anything."

"Oh. Well, I hope it's all right."

God, I'm such an idiot.

> *What's the problem?*

Didn't you hear me? I was so abrupt with her. She must have thought I hated her for sharing the table with Diana and me.

> *I don't think she would think that.*

That was my one chance to become friends with her and I totally blew it.

Harper made the tuna fish into a sandwich to take with her. She got up and put on her blazer. I had noticed that she always wore men's blazers. As she was leaving she said, "Good luck with your psych final Diana," in the sweetest voice. I observed that she left the sandwich on the table but didn't say anything.

After about fifteen minutes, Harper came back into the cafeteria laughing. "I forgot my sandwich." It made my heart ache to see her embarrassed. Then she left us for the second time.

I asked Diana about her and found out that she and Diana had known each other since they were little girls growing up in the same town in Connecticut. Diana said Harper was one of the sweetest people she knew. When I got back to the apartment, I decided to tell Carol that I thought she was wrong about "that neat-looking girl" being gay.

> *Do you want her to be gay?*

I don't know. It's probably safer if she's not. That way there's nothing I can do about it. I can kind of just enjoy looking at her and leave it at that.

> *Do you think it's wrong to do something about it?*

Yeah, that would make me really normal.

Still worried about being normal? I thought you would grow out of that by now.

Why would you think that?

You're learning to have a greater variety of friends—associate with different kinds of people. You're even starting to embrace your Asian heritage more.

Well, it helped me get into a good school, and Melanie kind of has a Japan fixation from her year living there. So, she's really interested in learning more about Asian culture and stuff. I just talk about being Chinese now because she's always asking me about it.

Did her questions make you sign up for Eastern Philosophy and East Asian history next year?

I don't think so.

Then why take those classes?

Maybe I am starting to think that it's not quite as bad as I always thought to be different—at least not from an ethnicity standpoint. But I'm really not sure it would extend as far being different, you know, in all ways. You can't ask too much from me all at once.

I took my first vacation home from college over the winter holidays. The month-long break back in suburban New Jersey bored me. I got together a couple of times with some of my high school friends, but things seemed different. Their normal, comfortable ways didn't interest me as much. I found myself thinking a lot about my new friends, with their punked-out hairdos and grungy clothes from secondhand stores. It occurred to me that it might actually be "cooler," or at least more commendable, to not be concerned about what other people think about you. So many of my new friends at college seemed to be like that, and they all impressed me with willingness—perhaps even yearning—to be seen as different. But I was still a long way from that myself. I looked forward to returning to college and being around my more eccentric and interesting friends, but allowed myself to fall back into the old patterns of my high school friendships during the break.

When I got back to school for my second semester of freshman year, I had an appreciation for the new friends I had made. But in spite of their individuality and unique qualities, I still didn't dare share anything about my crush on Harper. The only person I told about it that year was my brother Martin. I had written him one night when I was drunk, telling him that I had a "burning secret." Martin came to visit me during the spring break of his last semester at Swarthmore College. When he pressed me on the "burning secret" that I wrote about, I snuck him up to the TV lounge in my building. I didn't know how to come out and tell him my secret, so I asked him to guess.

"You're in love with someone," he ventured.

"Sort of."

"Is it Rob?" Rob was Martin's best friend in high school. I shook my head. He named some other boys I had known in high school and I kept shaking my head.

"It's not a guy," I finally said.

"It's a girl?"

"Yes."

"Who is it? Someone I've met here?"

"No," I explained. "I don't really know her. She's just someone that I see a lot. Or like to try to see."

"So, your 'burning secret' is a girl you like? That's kind of cute."

"You mean you don't think there's anything wrong with it?"

"I think it's okay to keep your options open at this point. You don't really have to decide about anything now. Maybe you like girls, or maybe it's just this particular girl."

I decided not to tell him about my crush on the girl I called Dog Face in junior high or the couple of other girls throughout my life I thought about that way. "You're probably right," I said. It was amazing to me that I had told someone, and my whole world hadn't fallen apart.

Do you feel better now that you've told someone?

You don't know how much.

Are you all right with it now?

Not quite. But now that Martin knows, and he didn't even judge me for it, maybe I don't have to feel so weird about it.

Martin is a generous boy. But why did you let him think that you're not sure about it?

Because I'm not. I know that Harper's not the only girl I ever felt like this about. But it doesn't mean that I'm ever going to do anything about it.

You might never do anything about it?

I mean, I might. Not yet, though. I'm just not totally comfortable with that idea yet.

Later in the second semester of freshman year, my new friends and I experimented with psychedelic drugs. Diana, Melanie, Jamie, and Alana had all experimented before and recommended trying new things to Carol and me. Carol's and my experiences before college were limited to marijuana. The first major thing Carol and I tried were hallucinogenic mushrooms, the kind used in some Native American spiritual rituals. I remember feeling a profound sense of loneliness and sorrow as I stared out the window and watched a stranger cross the street. It made me sad to think that I would never know the person I saw from my window—I would never know how she saw the world or what she was thinking. The thought nearly made me cry.

At the end of the school year, Jamie, Carol, and I split up a score of seven hits of acid. Alana, Jamie's roommate, had already dropped out of school by then and returned to Indiana, and Jamie announced that she had decided not to return the next year. By then, Carol had changed her mind about wanting to transfer to Yale and she was as sorry as I was that two of our closest friends would not be returning the following year. So as a farewell, we took the LSD with Jamie. I was not overwhelmingly impressed by the effect of the drug until late in the evening. We had dropped in to Diana's room to say goodbye and smoke some pot, when suddenly I desperately wanted to be alone. This time I was angry at the thought of not being able to know what other people were thinking. For several hours my anger convinced me that I never wanted to see another living human being again. But by the time Carol returned to our room just before dawn, the feeling had passed and I was glad to see her. The two of us went up to the roof of our building to watch the sunrise. In that early morning, a military truck carrying a giant missile passed beneath our view. We were left wondering if we had shared a hallucination that morning or if giant missiles were routinely transported through upper Manhattan in the early morning hours. I knew that we would probably remain friends for a long time.

> *What do these drugs do for you?*
> *Well, I don't think there's anything wrong with it. I'm not hurting anyone by taking drugs, after all.*
> *I didn't say you were. But are you learning anything?*
> *I don't know if it is from the drugs or just everything else about this year. But I do think I've learned stuff.*

What stuff?

It seems that we're all separate people and can't always be seen by other people the way we might like. And we all have these unique ideas or tastes that other people may not understand. But in a way though maybe the fact that we're all stuck in the same position—you know, share the same kinds of fears and feelings of aloneness—link us to each other in a more important way than our differences separate us.

That might be something.

PART 3

Minority me

CHAPTER 6

Orientation

In my second year at Barnard, I finally got to meet a bunch of lesbians. Ironically, it was indirectly through my friendship with my former seducer, Jose. For some reason, most likely to head off any new attempts to get me to sleep with him again, I chose Jose to be the second person I told that I thought I was gay. Jose acted supportive of the news but perhaps was a little too intrigued by it. He had a new girlfriend then and seemed to be hinting at a possible threesome. Neither his girlfriend, Laurie, nor I allowed Jose to completely verbalize his fantasy, so we avoided the awkward situation. But Laurie and I became friends. Laurie was the one who introduced me to a number of the openly gay women at the school.

There was Sofie, a short, heavy-set woman of mixed African-American and Jewish descent; Tracy, a tiny but surprisingly aggressive girl from Atlanta; Lauren, a tall, blond basketball player one year ahead of us; Nadya, a trendily dressed woman originally from Yugoslavia; Ursula, the daughter of an exiled leader from Somalia; and another girl named Jamie (not the one who dropped out after freshman year), who had short blond hair and always sported a black trench coat. I was amazed that I hadn't known any of these women in my first year and equally impressed that Laurie knew every one of them. While I continued my friendship with people I met freshman year, I started spending more time with this new group of Laurie's friends.

Now that I've actually met some lesbians, it's a bit strange. For so long, I thought that I was the only one who thought the way I did. It makes me a little scared. I don't seem to have the old excuses anymore that I couldn't possibly go through with anything. Other people have, and they lived through it.

It's a possibility now?

Yeah. But I'm still not sure it's what I want, because it's bound to make things more difficult for me.

Was it easy to pretend to be someone you weren't?

It wasn't that hard to pretend to like boys or even surrender to the pressure of having sex with guys. But I always felt kind of loathsome about it afterwards.

Maybe this is a better choice, then.

Though I became friends with these lesbians in my sophomore year, I still hadn't acted on my feelings. I told myself that I had a second chance at virginity. I knew that if I ever carried out my attraction toward a woman, it would have to be with someone I really cared for. For the majority of sophomore year, I was still consumed with my attraction to Harper—it bordered on obsession. I followed her from the supermarket one afternoon just to know which street she lived on. If I found her studying in the library, I would position myself at a table near her just so I could spend some time looking at her. I realized just how pathetic I had become one day when I saw her post a note on the cafeteria comment board. The note said, "Would love shrimp. There's a great brand called Shrimp Tahini." She signed it, "From a bunch of us." After she left, I snuck up to the board and stole the note as a memento. The next day I saw her look for a response on the comment board. When she couldn't find either her note or a response, she looked so disappointed. I felt disgusted with myself and made up my mind then that I had to do something.

I wrote Harper a letter and sent it to her campus mailbox. It's almost too embarrassing for me to try to remember exactly what I said in the note. I must have told her I was attracted to her and, while I didn't know her, I thought she seemed interesting. After writing the note, I felt somewhat liberated. I stopped panicking or trying to get up the nerve to talk to her when I would see her around campus. The ball seemed in her court now. A month passed and I got no response. Finally, I looked up her number in the phone book and gave her a call.

On the phone, she told me she hadn't gotten my letter, and she wasn't sure she knew who I was. But she was awfully nice on the phone, even though I must have sounded like an idiot trying to explain why I was calling her. She told me that I got her curious and that she wanted to get the letter from her mailbox and read it before going home for spring break. She said that, when she got back to school, she would give me a call and we could get together for coffee or something. I told myself that I had taken it as far as I could and felt proud of myself for having had the courage to follow through on my feelings.

That same week, I went home for spring break. When I was home, we went to visit my grandparents. They had moved out of our house after only living with us for a year. They moved to the apartment my uncle (their only son) had lived in before he and his wife bought a house following the birth of their daughter. As soon as my uncle had announced that he was moving to a house, Gnah Boo informed my mother that she would be moving too. While she lived with us, my grandmother constantly complained to her son about having to live with her youngest daughter. It wasn't for lack of space or privacy—by then my parents owned a twenty-room mansion where my grandparents had a whole wing to themselves—but Gnah Boo was hoping to live with her son. When my uncle bought a house, my grandmother naturally assumed that there would be room there for her and my grandfather, Gnah Kyong. By the time Gnah Boo discovered that my uncle, a busy and successful surgeon at a local hospital, never intended to have his parents live with him, she would not humiliate herself by asking my mother to let her stay. Instead, when my uncle and aunt moved out of their two-bedroom apartment, my grandparents took over its lease. My mother was just as happy to see her parents on the occasional visits to their apartment and at family dinners at our home.

They hadn't been long in the apartment when my grandmother started acting strangely. She had been forgetting things and was getting confused a great deal. Finally, she was diagnosed with Alzheimer's. When we went to visit them that spring break, my grandmother had almost completely forgotten how to speak English.

My grandfather opened the door for us. "Hello, hello," he greeted each one of us. "Good to see you."

"How is Mommy, eh?" my mother asked.

"Oh," he laughed. "Yesterday, she would not let me in the bed. She asked, 'Who are you, old man?' After fifty years! It's the most surprising thing."

Gnah Boo walked out from the bedroom, smiling and nodding to us. When she had lived with us she always took great pride in her appearance. She was dressed now in a robe. Her make-up looked sloppy and the grey roots were showing in her hair. "Hǎo ah, Mommy?" my mother asked her.

"Hǎo, Hǎo, Hǎo," she answered, bobbing her head up and down. She didn't look well to me.

"Sure, she's all right," my grandfather interrupted. "What does she know about it? I'm the one that knows."

My grandmother walked closer to me, with her head cocked to one side. "Yinghái," she said pointing at me and laughing.

"What is she saying?" I asked my mother.

"Baby, ha! Baby," Gnah Boo answered for me in English.

At first I thought that my grandmother was making a comment on my having gained weight since I was in college. Perhaps she thought I was pregnant. But my grandmother put her hands on my shoulders and, with a very happy voice, said, "Baby, baby."

"She doesn't know what she's saying," my grandfather offered. I had the eerie sense that she mistook me for her baby daughter that had died so many years earlier.

"Come look what I bought myself," my grandfather urged. He started leading us to the guest room to show us his new Tandy computer. My grandmother grabbed my mother by the arm to show her the area rug in the bedroom, in front of her vanity desk. She explained to my mother that the upstairs neighbor had snuck into their apartment and stolen her fine Oriental rug and replaced it with another rug of poor quality. My mother listened patiently.

"Computers are a very fine thing," my grandfather explained to us. "Now I can write my letters on the computer and write some essays on things that interest me. I think I would like to write an essay about why I do not believe in organized religion."

Gnah Kyong turned on the computer to demonstrate how it worked. At the blinking cursor, he tried typing a command. When he hit the enter button, the computer let out a beep and an error message appeared on the screen. "Oh," he apologized. "My first mistake."

"Huh! First mistake!" Came a mocking voice from the bedroom followed by an accusing laugh.

My grandfather looked embarrassed. Even with her Alzheimer's, his wife could still catch him in a lie. Reluctantly, Gnah Kyong took out the computer's instruction manual and looked up the correct commands.

Gnah Boo's still pretty funny. Even if she doesn't always know what's going on.

    Funny how?

You know, Gnah Kyong was trying to get away with something and Gnah Boo caught him and let him know that he wasn't being honest with himself.

    "First mistake." Do those words mean something to you?

It's a little like "original sin" from the story of Genesis 2–3.

    What was the "first mistake"?

It was when Eve ate the forbidden fruit.

    Why was it forbidden fruit?

It was fruit from the tree of the knowledge of good and evil.

    How was that a mistake?

Because it got Adam and Eve kicked out of the Garden of Eden, which was like paradise.

    Strange. Why would gaining knowledge be a mistake?

Beats me. I guess it's just an old story.

While I was home visiting my parents, I gathered them together around the kitchen table to tell them I was gay. It took me several minutes to muster the nerve to say anything.

"Did something happen?" my mother asked. The worry in her face was undeniable.

"No, it's nothing like that. I just wanted to share something with you. About me."

"What about you?" My father's voice was calmer, less panicked.

"It's just something I've figured out. You know... about who I really am. I mean... I think I'm gay." I waited for the fireworks. Ten seconds, twenty seconds, thirty seconds. It seemed like forever.

Finally, my father asked, "You think you are?"

"Well, I've never been with anyone. You know, a girl or anything. But I've always felt the attraction, ever since I can remember. I just didn't know what to call it until now. I thought it was something strange that only I felt. But now I know there are others like me out there. And maybe it's okay to be this way."

"It's those feminists at Barnard. They're the ones putting this in your head." My mother was already standing at the door leading up to her bedroom. "Nothing to discuss." And she was gone.

My father drove me back to the city and took me out to breakfast at a Cuban diner a few blocks south of my building.

"Mommy and I both love you," he told me. "You know that will never change. We hope you're not really gay, because that will be hard. Hard for you, I mean. But we will always love and support you, no matter what. Mommy may just need some time."

After I got back to school, I waited for Harper to call but she never did. Eventually, I called her. Over the phone, she told me, "I'm not gay or whatever, but I still think we should talk if you have feelings." It was the sweetest way to let me down. Somehow, after speaking to her, it didn't upset me that she never contacted me to talk about my feelings.

The act of writing the letter and confessing how she affected me felt like enough.

Events at Columbia that spring also helped take my mind off Harper. A flyer had drawn me to gather with about two hundred fellow students at the sundial in the middle of the campus plaza, organized by the student-led Coalition for a Free South Africa. We were promised speeches from the coalition steering committee urging the university to divest from all interests and investments in apartheid-plagued South Africa. The organizers told powerful stories about how apartheid, a system they explained literally meant "aparthood," segregated and oppressed the black and other non-white majority by white colonialists. They made us feel outrage over the imprisonment of Nelson Mandela since 1962. When the speeches were over, we were led on a march around campus, chanting and shouting. The march ended in front of Hamilton Hall, where the organizers suddenly chained and locked the front doors and announced they would remain there until the university committed to total divestment. Few of us in the crowd were expecting the bold action, but more than one hundred of us stayed to be part of the blockade. For me, it just felt right. There was the thrill and excitement from the threat that police might come at any moment to break us up. It alleviated some of my guilt from growing up privileged in a wealthy suburban American home. I felt like Don Quixote, taking a stand against our school's power structure to pressure a foreign government to end the injustice and immorality of apartheid. For three weeks, I spent all my time between classes at the encampment and sleeping outside the entrance to the building, which we had dubbed Mandela Hall during the blockade. When we finally disbanded after twenty-one days, the university had not yet agreed to divest from South African interests. However, our actions sparked a student movement that was replicated across the country. Five months later, Columbia University became the first American university to commit to fully divest from all stocks related to South Africa and, by 1988, another 155 educational institutions made similar divestment decisions. It would be nice to imagine that what we did that spring helped free Nelson Mandela and bring an end to apartheid.

I also started forgetting about Harper as I developed a crush on my new roommate, Allison. Allison was a transfer student from Vassar who moved in with me for the second semester of sophomore year. We shared a one-bedroom apartment at the College Residence Hotel on 110th Street. She was an attractive, tall woman, with one-quarter Chinese blood. Our relationship confused me. I confessed to Allison that I was gay, and she didn't seem to be bothered by it. She hugged me all the time and spoke sweetly to me. At Allison's suggestion, we even started sharing a bed (the pullout couch in the living room) by the middle of the semester. But Allison insisted that our relationship was only platonic. I thought it had to be otherwise. When she contradicted my belief by getting involved in relationships with various men, I was angry and hurt by it. I couldn't yet distinguish between a physically affectionate friendship with a woman and sexual intimacy with one. It very nearly ruined our friendship.

This is crazy! Falling for straight women is really confusing. And painful.

Aren't there ways to find others like you?

Sure. There are student groups, bars, and places like that. I guess if I'm going to be gay, then I should look for another woman who's gay to be with.

That might be interesting.

Chapter 7

A SECOND CHANCE
AT VIRGINITY

We met at a bar. My friends always told me never to expect to meet someone at a bar, but that's why we go to them. Something I said caught Caroline's attention.

"I have trouble expressing myself to other people." I was talking to my freshman housemate, Melanie, sitting next to me, but Caroline picked up on the conversation.

"Why do you have trouble talking to people? Is it because you think you're smarter than everyone else?"

"Excuse me?"

I had barely seen Caroline burst through the front door of the Sheridan Square nightclub and rush past me on her way to the bathroom. When she pulled up a stool beside me, I was facing my friend in the opposite direction. I didn't want to seem predatory by turning around to check her out.

"What are you saying?" Caroline pressed. When I realized she was, in fact, addressing me, I turned around to face her. "That you think that no one will understand you?" she asked. Her smile and the faint lines around her eyes made me think that she didn't mean it in a vicious way—she was being playful. Still, I was thrown by the interruption.

"No, that's not it. I don't know why."

"It's okay, I understand," she answered, still smiling. "I used to be the same way. Well... actually, I'm still the same way." She placed her hand on my shoulder in a friendly, comforting way. The warmth of her hand was very pleasant.

Caroline was tall and thin with neatly styled short blond hair. Even in the bar's light I could make out that her eyes were green with tiny flecks of amber outlining the pupils. When she smiled at me, her eyes lit up and seemed to penetrate my usually private world. She was wearing dark eyeliner and bright red lipstick, something I usually found less appealing. But underneath the makeup she looked wholesome and athletic in her blue jeans, white dress shirt, and black leather jacket. I was instantly attracted to her.

> *You really like this Caroline, Sya Meh?*
>
> *I think so. She's so beautiful. Except for the makeup, she looks just like the kind of woman I always dreamed of being with. And it seemed so easy for me to talk to her. You know how hard it is for me to meet people—especially in that kind of situation. But something just seemed to click between us.*
>
> *What is clicked?*
>
> *It just seemed kind of funny that the two of us—complete strangers— wanted to talk to each other about how difficult it is for us to talk to other people. But maybe that's what makes the whole thing special.*
>
> *Do you think she got the joke?*
>
> *I know she did. And it was a private one, just between us.*

On the following night, we were supposed to meet outside the movie theater, but I felt nervous about the arrangements. What if she didn't show up? I didn't want to look foolish waiting in front of a theater for someone who would never show. So, I surprised her by going directly to her hotel room. She had given me the name and phone number of the hotel where she was staying, explaining that she just moved back to the city a few days earlier and had not yet found an apartment. Despite the surprise, she smiled broadly when she opened the door and hugged me in front of the door. Facing each other standing, no longer on our bar stools, I could see just how tall Caroline was—over six feet, towering over me by nearly a foot. I also saw that it wasn't the alcohol or the bar's dim lighting that made me think she was so attractive. The heavy makeup from the night before was all washed away, and the natural color of her lips, face, and eyes made her even more beautiful to me.

As we walked to the theater a few blocks away, Caroline explained what was in store for the evening.

"We're going to meet someone else at the theater, this woman Florence. I met her after you left. You don't mind, do you?"

Had she actually arranged a double date with just her and two women? If she had been looking at my face when she told me, she might have seen my mortification. But I made sure my voice didn't betray me.

"Of course not," I assured her. "That's fine with me."

After the movie, the three of us went to a small café and had drinks. I was amazed at my lack of shyness and my ability to speak freely without tripping on my words. The other woman we were with was indeed named Florence, but she wanted to change her name to Felicia.

"You've got to be kidding. Felicia?" I laughed. Caroline doubled over in laughter too.

Florence looked confused and she might have even been holding back tears as her eyes passed between Caroline and me laughing at her. "What's wrong with Felicia?"

It pleased me to make Caroline laugh. "I mean Florence is bad enough. But Felicia? It sounds like something a rodent would scream if you stepped on its tail. Fel-EEEE-sha!" I squealed. Caroline slapped the table in approval.

Florence was having trouble keeping up with the conversation. She was Haitian, and it seemed to take her a moment to translate the thoughts in her head from French to English before she could share them with us. In the meantime, I monopolized the conversation with Caroline. I told her about Echo the bunny that lived in the kitchen pantry of my freshman year apartment suite. Echo would lead us on chases through the apartment that inevitably ended with his peeing on one of our beds. I told her about my beagle, who solved his constipation problem by yelping a high-pitched bark. And how sometimes I'd hear my brother in the bathroom trying to copy the dog's remedy. By midnight, Caroline slid over in the booth so she sat directly across from me at the table. Even when Florence thought of something to say, she'd have to keep repeating it to get Caroline to hear it. I didn't mind when Florence gave up trying.

When we left the café, I thought of one more trick to get rid of Florence. There was a subway station directly across the street from the café. As soon as we stepped out onto the sidewalk I asked Florence how she planned to get home. After hesitating a moment, she committed herself to taking the subway and asked if I wanted to take it with her.

"No, I think I'll walk uptown a couple of blocks to catch the crosstown bus." I knew that Caroline would have to walk uptown to get to her hotel. Caroline and I said goodbye to Florence, and I was pleased with my cleverness when I saw her disappear down into the subway station.

"Do you mind if I walk uptown with you for a little ways?" I asked Caroline.

"I'd like that."

At Eighty-Sixth Street, a block from her hotel, we reached an Irish Pub. "It's not too late for you to have another drink with me, is it?" Caroline asked. My persistence had paid off. We sat down at a table for two in the middle of the pub. The room was a large square with a high ceiling. Bright fluorescent lights hung from the ceiling, dimmed only by the cigarette smoke that blanketed the room.

Caroline relaxed in her chair across from me. "That Florence kind of made me nervous. I think I feel much more comfortable with you." I fought to keep from smiling too much.

We ordered a pitcher of Irish ale to share. Caroline took out a cigarette from a pack of Red Rothman's and offered me one. I pulled out my Zippo lighter and showed off how I could snap the lighter open between my thumb and two fingers and light it in a quick, fluid motion. It felt like the most natural thing in the world to be drinking, smoking, and talking with Caroline.

At one point in the conversation, Caroline asked, "If you were in love with someone and they didn't love you back, would you give up?"

"I don't think I could," I answered. I was sure that I wasn't lying, even though I had never been in love. I liked the question, despite the fact that I suspected that she was thinking about someone other than me.

"I can't either," Caroline sighed. Then she leaned closer to me and shot me a mischievous smile. "So, who was that you were with at the bar last night?"

"Oh, that was just Melanie, one of my freshman housemates. She's not gay but sometimes she likes to pretend she is. She thinks it makes her more artistic or something. She did have an affair with a woman once. But basically, she just likes sex."

"She's not your girlfriend then?"

"No," I said quickly. "I could never. We're just friends. I like her a lot because she's kind of a unique person. Except that sometimes I think she lies just to get attention."

"Lies about what?"

"Well, out of the blue recently she claimed that she was raped by her adopted brother when she was younger. I have a hard time believing it."

Caroline's voice took on a sharp edge. "Why wouldn't you believe her? I believe her."

"What do you mean? You don't even know Melanie."

Caroline ignored my question. "My brother molested me too. My real brother. I was five and he was eight. And it lasted for a long time, 'til I finally got out of the house at thirteen." She snuffed out a cigarette that was barely smoked. Then she grabbed my lighter off the table, lit a new cigarette, and threw the lighter back towards me. It bounced once on the table and hit me just below the chin.

"I'm so sorry, Caroline. I didn't mean anything by it. It's not like I don't believe that kind of thing happens. It was just coming from her. You know, Melanie likes to shock sometimes for effect. But I'm really sorry about you. And of course, I believe you."

As Caroline's face relaxed and she smiled again, I could see that she had been afraid.

"Never mind. I'm sorry I brought it up." We were through with the subject. Caroline was upbeat for the rest of the night, and we found plenty of other things to talk and laugh about until the bar closed down.

Caroline gave me a hug when we stepped outside. "I had a good time tonight," she told me. "You think you'd want to do something again with me sometime?"

"Sure," I answered, trying not to sound too eager.

"How about Monday?" She laughed. It was only two days away. "Sorry. Is that too soon?"

What could she have to worry about? I accepted her invitation without any hesitation.

I might have hidden the depth of my attraction if I had not gone to see her the very next day. Caroline didn't seem surprised or upset when I showed up at her hotel room. Spontaneously, we spent the day together. We had cappuccino at a café on the East Side and rode the bus across town to a flea market on Columbus Avenue. She helped me pick out a fancy antique hat that looked like it might have belonged to a flapper and she bought some old-looking black-and-white postcards of New York. I took her to meet my brother, who had moved to the city after graduating from Swarthmore, and I introduced her to my infamous beagle, Caleb, who was living with Martin at the apartment. The three of us had an early dinner at a Mexican restaurant on Broadway. Before we parted, Caroline reminded me of our date the next day to see a movie together (as if I needed reminding). She genuinely seemed to enjoy my company, and I was convinced that I was falling in love with her.

On our second planned date, I waited outside the theater for her. Twenty minutes after the movie had started, it seemed my worst fears were being realized. She was standing me up. I was about to leave when I saw her running towards me.

"Hey! Sorry. I guess we missed the start of the movie." She was breathing heavily from running. I could smell liquor on her breath. "Would you mind skipping the movie thing and just going out for cocktails? I already started, you know."

"Sure, whatever you want," I said. "I don't care so much about the movie. I'm just glad you showed up. I really wanted to see you again."

"Aw, that's sweet." She patted me on the back. Her legs were a lot longer than mine and she was taking big steps in a rush towards her cocktails. I had to walk quickly to keep up with her. We stopped at another Irish pub on West Seventy-Ninth Street.

The Dublin House was more intimate than the pub from the night before. The lights were dim, and the front section of the pub was narrow. There were no tables, only bar stools lined up along the bar and against the mirrored walls with hanging bar counters.

"Let's get something stronger tonight," Caroline urged. "I'll have a cognac," she told the bartender. Then turning to me, "And you? It'll be my treat, okay?"

"I guess I'll have a vodka tonic."

"That's getting there."

By the time we got seats by the wall opposite the bar, Caroline had finished her glass of cognac. "Ready for another?" she asked.

"Not quite!" I gestured to my full glass.

"Well, hurry up and finish. And then you can do away with the tonic. Let's just do shots, okay?"

"I don't know, Caroline."

"Come on. Show me what they've been teaching you at that fancy college of yours."

I kept up with Caroline for four quick shots. And I was feeling it. It seemed to loosen Caroline up, too. Finally, she told me what was on her mind.

"I'm not who you think I am," she began.

"What do you mean?"

"I'm going to tell you some things about me tonight that are going to make you change your mind about me."

"I don't believe that," I protested.

"I'm not what you want. There are a lot of things about my past that you just don't know. You're a good person. And I'm not who you want."

What she was saying didn't make any sense—I couldn't understand it. I pressed her to explain it to me. She rolled up her sleeves and showed me her arms.

"Do you know what these are?"

I had never seen anyone with them before, but I guessed that they were track marks. I couldn't think of anything to say.

"I was a fucking junkie," she said after a while. She waited for my reaction.

"It doesn't matter," I told her finally. "It doesn't change how I feel about you."

"How can you say that? I don't think you understand. These marks won't ever go away. I can never wear a short-sleeved shirt without everyone seeing that I was a fucking junkie. Look at my arms. Do you see them?"

I saw, but I answered again, "It doesn't matter."

"Okay then. Well, you already know about what happened with my brother. But that's not all. I've also had two kids, two boys. Gave them both up for adoption three years apart before I was eighteen. And I also worked as a working girl. You know what that means, don't you? Is that who you really want?"

I couldn't think of anything to say.

"What's wrong with you? I'm twenty-three years old and I've already had two kids and used to be a junkie and prostitute. Listen, I'm no good. I'm trouble. You don't want to get involved with me."

"Caroline, I can save you."

Save her? Really?

I know. It's kind of a corny thing to say.

Not corny, Sya Meh. Maybe not true.

Maybe it can be true.

What do you know about the things she's described?

I know enough to know that it wasn't her fault. I'm not denying that she's had a hard life and done some unpleasant things. I don't think I should give up someone I really care about just because of her past. I can tell that she's not a bad person. I think she's just ashamed of what happened to her before she was old enough to take care of herself. That's probably why she's had all that trouble with sex and drugs. But I can help her. I can make her see that she's not a bad person, just because bad things happened to her.

Be careful with this, Sya Meh. You could get hurt.

We'll be good together, Ah Kung. You'll see. It'll all work out.

Caroline leaned her head on my shoulder. "Gosh, you really are sweet." She took my left hand and twirled the ring I wore on my ring finger around between her thumb and index finger. Gently, she pulled the ring off. She held my wrist with one hand, then slipped the ring back on my finger.

"You know I really do like you," she said. "Would it be all right if I kissed you?"

I was oblivious to the people drinking around us. This was not a safe environment, but I didn't care. We left the bar shortly after and took a subway up to my dorm room.

What if you're right and I've made a mistake, Ah Kung? What if I got myself mixed up in all this and I don't really love her?

— 92 —

Was it less than you imagined it would be?

No, not that. That was great. Better than I ever imagined really. But with Caroline, it's not just about that for me. I'm not thinking about this as a one-night stand like with so many guys I've been with. When I was finally with a woman, I wanted it to be someone I was in love with. I'm definitely attracted to her and I have really strong emotions when I'm around her. I'm just not sure what they are.

What emotions?

Pity maybe. Insecurity. Being possessive too. But at the same time, I feel confident and cared about when I'm around her. Like for the first time someone sees in me what I have to offer.

You're not willing to give it up yet then?

Definitely not. I don't know how it will all work out, but I want to keep going.

In the morning, Caroline was incredibly tender. She kissed me on the forehead before getting out of bed and opening up the window to smoke a cigarette. The sun was reflecting a golden glow off the Hudson River. Caroline leaned her head out the window to get a better view.

She slipped her head back inside. "Would it be all right if I fell in love with you?"

"I'd like it if you did," I answered.

"Okay then. I think I will."

You see, Ah Kung? Everything's going to be all right.

CHAPTER 8

TOO GOOD TO BE TRUE

I read the tiny sliver of paper out loud and let a nervous laugh escape. "If it seems too good to be true, it probably is."

"What did it say?" my brother Martin asked.

I was sure he heard me the first time and didn't repeat it. He peered over my shoulder to see the scrap of paper in my hand. "Hm, that's an interesting fortune."

"I don't believe in this kind of thing," I insisted. "It's not like I'm going to worry about what a fortune cookie says."

Is that true? You of all people take those things to heart.

Not really. Besides, I don't see anything that's too good to be true. It's all good.

Doesn't it seem like your friend is hiding something from you?

No. If anything, she's been too honest. And I'm having the time of my life.

The days were getting longer, the air was warming up, and everything seemed unbelievably clear that March in New York. The trees that popped out of the cement sidewalks were no longer bare and it was pleasant to be outside. When it rained, New York had the same musty smell that always reminded me of the spring, but when the rain was over, there was a cleanness and crispness to the city that you didn't experience at any other time of the year.

I waved to the hotel clerk who I thought would recognize me from my frequent visits to Caroline. But he made me stop at the desk and sign in as he called Caroline to let her know I was coming up. I held the elevator for a man who had entered the hotel a little after me. He didn't stop at the receptionist's desk so I assumed he was a guest.

The man looked at the elevator panel and saw that the button for the sixth floor was already lit from when I had pressed it.

"Oh," he said, but pressed the button again anyway.

He allowed me to exit first when we reached our floor and followed me toward the same end of the hallway. When I knocked on Caroline's door, the man was standing right behind me.

Caroline stared at us with a strange expression as we both stood outside her room. I thought she looked panicked. "What's going on?" she asked suspiciously.

"What do you mean?" I asked, confused by the question.

"Oh, you mean you both just came to see me at the same time, ha ha ha." She sounded relieved. And it amused me that she was the first person I ever met that actually laughed using the word "ha."

I turned to the man who was still standing right behind me. "You're here to see Caroline too?"

"Um, yes. I am"

"Ha, ha" Caroline laughed again as she let us both into the room. "This is Bill. My Uncle Bill. He's just here to help me get things settled. You know, so I can move out of this hotel. He's helping me with money. I mean, he's helping me get money out of my trust. Or I should really say get the money my parents don't trust me with."

I hadn't noticed any family resemblance and looked back at the man standing behind me to check what I had missed. He was a short, stocky man. He didn't seem more than a few inches taller than I, which would still leave him a half-foot shorter than Caroline. His hair was dark but beginning to gray, making it seem a dull, almost charcoal color. It seemed a stark contrast to Caroline's blond hair, though it had occurred to me that she might dye it. His features were rounded and he had rough, tanned skin that had a leathered quality from years of sun exposure. In all, he gave me the impression of being of Mediterranean origin—Italian or Greek. I never would have guessed a familial relationship with Caroline.

Bill looked annoyed. I figured that he didn't like Caroline sharing details about their family issues.

Caroline noticed his expression too. "It's okay, Uncle Bill." Her voice seemed more teasing than reassuring. "This is my new friend. She's nice and she doesn't mind meeting me here at the hotel. But it'll be so much nicer once I move into my own apartment. So you got the apartment, right?"

"Yes, I put down the deposit today. That's what I stopped by to tell you. I couldn't get through to you on the phone."

"And you'll help me get my things out of storage and moved into the new place?" she asked.

"I already told you I would, Caroline." Bill responded, still sounding annoyed.

"Of course you did." Caroline smiled. "I'm just so happy to be moving to a real apartment again. I just wanted to be sure everything's take care of. And no roommates this time either. You're so good to me, Bill. Uncle Bill. But you're not planning on staying, are you? 'Cause I think that my new friend wants to go out with me tonight." She turned to me questioningly.

"Yeah, I thought we would. But if you're busy…"

"No, you called and made an appointment with me tonight. My Uncle Bill just stopped by unannounced."

"No, I won't stay," Bill confirmed. "But I…" He seemed to be searching for words.

"You have money for me?" Caroline asked slyly.

"Yes."

"Oh good. Then we can have a wonderful time tonight!" She was looking at me now.

Bill took out his silver money clip. "I'm going to give you two hundred dollars now," he whispered to Caroline. "Well, for now. But be good though. You know what I mean."

"Don't you just love how my uncle worries about me?"

"All right, Caroline." He said it in a way that sounded like he wanted to add "that's enough."

Caroline laughed. It was clear that she wasn't taking his annoyance very seriously.

"Well, you need to meet me at the realtor's tomorrow at two, Caroline. It's no joke now. You have to show up to sign the lease if you want the apartment."

"Of course. I'll be there. Don't worry Uncle Bill. You know that I want to move into my own place, so I can entertain guests properly and all. Here at the hotel, you know, it's really not at all convenient to entertain. But you really should be going now. I'll see you tomorrow at two." She opened the door and ushered Bill to the hallway.

Bill hesitated. I sensed he wanted to speak to Caroline privately. But she was very cleverly not allowing him any opening to do so. Caroline pulled me further into the room and closed the door behind us, leaving Bill on the other side. She peered through the peephole with a look of amusement. She turned back toward me finally after I figured she saw Bill climb back into the elevator.

"I'm really glad you were able to come by tonight," she told me. "I think we really need to talk."

"Talk about what?" The words and her tone surprised me.

"Well, we've been spending a lot of time together recently, since we met. And I do sincerely enjoy your company."

"I'm glad," I said. I hoped she couldn't detect my insecurity. "I really enjoy your company too."

"Yeah, I know. Hey, I'm going to get a drink. Do you want one?"

"Sure."

Caroline crossed the room to the miniature refrigerator. From the outside, the hotel looked more like a regular apartment building than most of the hotels I had seen in Manhattan. But the mini-bar looked like one you would find in any other hotel, and the dirty mustard-colored carpet and brown and orange floral-patterned bedspread gave it away.

"You can have a seat, you know. We're not formal here." She pointed toward the bed.

I sat at the edge of the bed rather uncomfortably. My feet were still planted on the ground and I had nowhere to lean back.

"Here you go."

I was surprised when Caroline handed me a ginger ale rather than something alcoholic. Caroline sat down next to me on the bed but leaned back confidently, resting herself on her elbow for a moment. Then she pulled herself back upright.

"What I'm trying to say is that I really do like you." She rested her hand familiarly on my leg, just above the knee. "I mean, I think we really get along well. And I think maybe we even love each other. But as intellectual friends, you know. I don't think it's what you think it is between us."

She waited for me to say something. My throat felt like something was stuck in it. I swallowed but the feeling remained. Maybe it was my words that were stuck there.

"Well this is kind of serious… difficult stuff. I think we should get stoned for this conversation, don't you?"

I shrugged my shoulders, leaving it up to her. I didn't particularly like marijuana. It always made me feel uncomfortable in my mind and body and it often made me paranoid. But I knew Caroline was crazy for it. She wasn't waiting for my agreement anyway. She had already made her way from the bed to the top drawer of the hotel dresser and pulled out a black leather pouch.

She returned to the bed with the parcel and her pack of imported cigarettes. From the side pocket of the pouch she retrieved a small pack of rolling papers and laid two papers on the leg of her blue jeans. She licked the adhesive end of one of the papers and attached it to the second paper. She creased the papers near where they were attached and balanced the now V-shaped paper on her thigh. The larger pocket of the pouch held a plastic ziplock bag with several buds of marijuana. She took out one large bud and pinched it in both hands and twisted it in half, returning one half to the baggy. I watched Caroline expertly crumple the remaining half of the bud over the paper so that it fell into the crease. She picked out the few seeds and a small stem that fell into the paper and put them back into the plastic bag. Keeping the still-incomplete joint on her thigh, she opened her pack of cigarettes and pulled one cigarette out. She rolled the cigarette between her thumb and index finger with the open end over the papers so that about half the tobacco fell into the paper. Then she rolled it using the friction from her jeans and licked the wide end of the paper to seal it. It wasn't the delicate rolling procedure that I had seen other people perform and wasn't anything like the way I had worked so hard to master rolling loose-tobacco cigarettes. But it was efficient and packed a surprisingly nice-looking joint.

She lit it and took a deep drag, holding it in as long as she could. She handed it to me and I did the same. The tobacco made it smoother than other joints I had smoked and neither of us had to cough. After a few more drags, I felt the familiar pasty dryness envelop my mouth and my limbs felt somehow detached from my body. When I turned towards Caroline, she was looking at me with an expression that seemed to be true affection.

I swear, Ah Kung. She wants me to kiss her.

Aren't you listening?

Look at how she's looking at me! I'm sure she loves me just a little bit.

Yes. But she also told you it's not the way you think.

Maybe she just doesn't understand how she loves me. Or maybe she's just trying to deny her true feelings. She could even be trying to protect me. She probably still thinks that she's no good and that she'd be trouble for me.

She could be right.

As I leaned in to kiss her, Caroline leaned over too and met my lips with her own.

"Um," she moaned. She was on top of me on the bed in an instant, her body pressing itself against me. Her kisses were insistent, and her hands felt under my clothes to touch my skin.

She came quickly, with our clothes still on. She gave me one last deep kiss and rolled off me to lean on her side and smiled.

"Well, there's nothing wrong with intellectual friends that love each other making love on occasion, is there?" Her eyes wandered around the room. "You know this lousy hotel reminds me of a place I once worked in as a call girl."

She told me the story of a famous Hollywood director who hired Caroline and another girl and forced them to lie perfectly still, naked on a bed while he went down on them. He wouldn't let them make any sound or movement, as if they were drugged or dead perhaps. Then he asked the girls to act like puppets as he directed them in a sex scene with each other.

I started thinking that it was interesting that this particular director hired prostitutes to act out sexual perversions and his desire to direct sex, since graphic sex was conspicuously absent in all of his movies.

> *Why worry about that director? Shouldn't your friend's story about being a prostitute be more concerning?*
>
> *I guess I'm not all that surprised by it. I think a lot of incest survivors fall into prostitution.*
>
> *And it doesn't bother you?*
>
> *I don't want to judge her. I don't know what it's been like for her having to go through all the pain she's lived with.*
>
> *Couldn't that just be an excuse for bad behavior?*
>
> *Not an excuse. I just think that there's a strange logic to it. It makes a certain kind of sense from a psychological standpoint. When she was*

only five, her brother forced her to have sex. In a way, he stole her body from her. So when she got older, she made the conscious choice not to let anyone steal her body again. Instead she would sell it, so that she could have some control over things. I'm not saying that it's right. I just don't think I can judge her for it. After all, Jesus stood up for a prostitute too.

But didn't Jesus also tell her something else?

Yeah, he said "go and sin no more." She's told me she's not doing that anymore.

You don't think there's something strange with her uncle?

That's sick, Ah Kung. No, I don't think her uncle is paying her to have sex with him.

Well, something's not right here.

Caroline and I spent a lot of time together that spring, both outside and indoors. She took me up to the Cloisters Museum in Fort Tryon Park. We picnicked on French bread and Brie cheese and a bottle of Italian Chianti on the grounds, overlooking the river, before touring the museum. We took long walks in Central and Riverside Parks and window shopped along Broadway. We saw a double feature of Federico Fellini movies at the revival movie theater on Ninety-Sixth Street. And when the day was over, we would often go to a bar or pub and drink and smoke cigarettes until the early morning hours. Sometimes our outing would end at my dorm room, sometimes her apartment, and sometimes we'd just part company. I never knew how the night would wind up until Caroline announced her decision at the end of the evening.

I liked being with Caroline at her new apartment. It felt very grown up. Caroline's was the only real New York City apartment that I had spent any substantial time in.

One evening I was on my way to her apartment, feeling quite excited and content. The M104 bus was bright and clean and I knew that it had just recently been put into service. It transported me downtown, taking me past familiar sights on Broadway—the bars I frequented as a freshman and sophomore, the College Residence Hotel where I lived during my sophomore year, Chun Cha Fu Restaurant on Ninety-Second Street where my parents used to take my brother and me for birthday banquets, and other places I could walk to from school. Caroline and I were going to go to my first political rally in Washington, DC. It was Caroline's idea—she was the one who suggested that I buy the tickets for both of us. But I was happy to be going. I had stayed away from the political rallies some of my friends went to when I was in high school. Back then the issue was nuclear disarmament. While I agreed with the cause, there wasn't much of an opposition contingency, so it never seemed all that exciting to me. But this was a pro-choice, abortion rights rally. I knew there were plenty of people on the other side of the issue, so it seemed important for Caroline and me to take part. The bus was scheduled to leave from the Columbia campus, but Caroline had asked me to pick her up at her apartment and then she would get us a cab back to campus. I didn't mind the extra effort to pick her up. I had taken to making sure of my plans with Caroline in person, since she still didn't have a phone.

At Eighty-Sixth Street I got off the M104 and took a crosstown bus to the East Side, through Central Park. This bus was an older model, covered in graffiti, with seats that squeaked when you sat on them. I pulled the cord to stop the bus just before reaching Third Avenue. The sun had set an hour or so earlier, but it was always easy to make your way around in the evening in New York. I pushed the door open when the buzzer sounded. The walk up to Caroline's fourth floor, which I took two steps at a time, warmed me up. I took a few deep breaths with my mouth wide open so I wouldn't seem out of breath before I knocked on the door.

Caroline opened the door but barely acknowledged me as she frantically searched around the apartment. It was a modest-sized studio with the main living area about twenty feet by thirty feet in all. The carpet was light blue with a medium shag pile and the walls were painted in simple white. Because the building was only a single apartment wide and there was a narrow alley between it and the next building to its east, Caroline's apartment had windows on three sides. It had a skylight too, but there was a crack in it, so it was covered with a blue tarp. Her bed was a pine-colored lightly finished wood IKEA queen-sized frame, and the mattress sat on slats set across the frame with no box spring. She had bookshelves on two sides of the studio, one filled with books by authors ranging from Oscar Wilde and Albert Camus to Rita Mae Brown, and the other where she set up her Walkman and stereo speakers. The kitchenette was equipped with fairly modern appliances—a white refrigerator and chrome electric oven and stove. A bar separated the kitchenette from the living area. A medium-sized square table, which matched the wood of the bed, sat in front of the west-facing window and constituted her dining area.

On the dining table, there was a small tinted glass vial of cocaine or heroin, I didn't know which. Its black screw-on top was lying on the table next to it. The apartment looked like Caroline had torn the place apart looking for something, but the drugs were sitting on the table in plain view. It dawned on me that she was searching for something to help her use the drugs. She was searching for needles.

I had the urge to grab the vial away from her. But I sat still, watching her from a stool by the kitchen counter.

You should just get out of here now.

No, I have to stay.

   Are you just going to stay and watch this?

How can I stop her if that's really what she wants to do?

   Then what's the use of your staying?

If Caroline hadn't already taken drugs, it seemed obvious that she had indulged in at least one, if not both, of the bottles of red wine that sat on the dining table next to the vial. After she finished emptying her dresser drawers onto the floor and rummaging through the clothes that fell out, she swayed until she straightened herself and walked clumsily toward the dining table. She fell back into one of the chairs by the table, a wooden folding chair, and had to catch her balance by grabbing the table. As she did so, the vial toppled over and began slowly to roll toward the edge of the table. I watched it roll and then fall, as if in slow motion, spilling the contents of the vial onto the shag carpet.

I expected Caroline to go crazy, losing what was most likely an expensive vial of drugs. But she didn't even seem to notice what she had done. I was relieved that Caroline was so out of it that there was no need for me to attempt to take away the drugs. She just laughed at the mishap.

When she finished laughing, she got up and started to change her clothes. "I'm going out and you'll come with me."

I nodded.

"We'll dance for a while," she mumbled to me.

"And then what?"

"Then I'll be yours."

I looked at my feet.

She headed into the bathroom and looked at herself in the mirror, considering her makeup. "You know my old girlfriend always told me that I only go after people I know I can get."

"You mean like me?" I asked, not wanting to hear the answer.

She stopped gazing at her reflection to stare back into my eyes. "Yeah, just like you."

Caroline returned looking at her reflection in the mirror. "Who are you?!" she screamed. "I don't know you!"

Then she looked at me again. "I'm what you people would call attractive." A stream of drool was dripping down her chin.

You still think she is attractive this way?

No, not like this.

Then when are you going to make a decision?

I have to see this through!

After putting some makeup on sloppily all over her face, she grabbed her coat and walked into the hallway outside her apartment, letting the door close behind her with me still inside.

As she predicted, I went with her and abandoned the rally. We ended up at a women's dance club in the East 50s. The dance floor was crowded and Caroline kept bumping into people as she danced with abandon. I did my best to apologize to the angry women she kept bumping into, protecting her from their wrath. Finally, the manager came over and told me Caroline had to leave and helped me get her out of the club without a scene. I was glad that Caroline hardly seemed to be aware of what was happening. When we got back to Caroline's apartment, she said I was being too protective and I could just get the hell out. Then she told me she never wanted to see me again.

"Go to Washington and leave me alone. I already have a mother and I don't need another."

I left, but I didn't go to Washington. Instead I waited in the lobby of a nearby bank until morning and went back to Caroline's to see if she was all right. For about three hours I waited outside her apartment building in the cold morning air and sporadically rang her buzzer. There was no way to tell whether she was home or not but ringing the buzzer gave me something to do. Around noontime she finally came to the intercom and asked angrily, "Who is it?" I answered back, almost as angrily, "It's me. Let me up." She buzzed me in and I ran up the stairs.

As I entered her apartment I asked her, "Are you going to be a junkie for the rest of your life?"

"Probably," she answered.

"Why are you so stupid? Can't you see I'm trying to help you?"

"Well, I guess I'm just stupid. What do you want from me?"

"I think I have a right to talk to you when you're not high."

"Look, I didn't get high last night. Really. I was just drunk. Come on, why don't you just come in, sit down, and have a cigarette. We'll talk, okay?"

She told me that she couldn't remember most of what had happened the night before and assured me that she couldn't recall telling me that she never wanted to see me again. Her voice was gentle and she seemed sad rather than angry.

"I don't know, Bill came by and gave me money last night. And I was feeling kind of bad about myself."

"So how come your Uncle Bill gives you money, anyway?"

"I told you all about this before, didn't I?"

"No, I don't think so." She must have told someone else she'd been spending time with.

"Oh, well you know I have this trust fund, you see, from my parents. But obviously they don't trust me with it. You know, they're afraid I'll use the money for drugs or something. So they go through my Uncle Bill to get money to me. They won't let me have a lot at any one time."

"But you did use it for drugs. I saw the vial last night."

"Well, that wasn't much. What business is it of yours anyway?" Then more gently, "Really, the money he gave me was for me to get a phone and to get some more of my things out of storage. But it makes me feel kind of down when I have to get money from Bill."

Does that sound right to you? Why would having a trust fund make someone want to drink or do drugs?

It does seem a bit extreme. But maybe the fact that no one seems to trust her, including me, makes her feel depressed.

Something else is going on here. Why don't you go home to your family for a while? Let yourself spend a little time away from her and see if you feel differently.

My mother had asked me to come home for a few days for spring break, as if she sensed I was getting myself too deep into something. Before leaving for home, I stopped by Caroline's place to tell her that I wouldn't be around for a few days. She still hadn't gotten a phone, so I had to go by in person to tell her. It was four thirty in the afternoon and Caroline had already finished over half a bottle of wine by herself.

"Can you keep me company for a little while?" she asked.

"Well, I'm supposed to meet my father at the train station at six."

"I'm feeling kind of down again. And being with you makes me feel better about myself."

"Okay, I can stay for one glass of wine."

"I guess I'll take what I can get." She brought another glass from the kitchen and poured me a full glass of Chianti. "I really like spending time with you, even though we're from really different worlds. It's kind of like I'm John Lennon and you're Yoko Ono."

I thought about pointing out the racist aspect of the Yoko Ono comparison but let it go.

"It's nice that you get along with your family. You ever read the book Toxic Parents? That's what it's like when I go home. And I guess your brother's a lot different from mine."

I felt my heart break for her. I couldn't imagine what it would be like to have a brother abuse me.

"Well, never mind that. I'm happy for you that you're going home."

"Thanks." I sipped up the last bit of wine from my glass.

"Before you go, do you think you could lend me twenty dollars? Bill's late coming by with my money."

"Of course I can."

"You're a doll."

Caroline walked me to the subway station. "When you get back I'll give you a call and we can have dinner or something." She gave me a hug and it felt so warm and comfortable with her long arms and leather jacket that stretched out like bat wings wrapped around me. "You know I'm going to miss you," she said nervously. "I really want to see you when you get back, okay?"

"Definitely," I said and kissed her on the lips. "I'll wait for your call."

"That's a date," she laughed and kissed me once again before I ran down to catch the subway.

While I was home I didn't talk to my family about my new relationship. But I thought about Caroline nearly every minute of every day.

You still think you love her after her most recent behavior?

If anything, missing her so much makes me feel like I love her even more.

But you know you'll get hurt, don't you?

I have to take that chance, Ah Kung. I feel that she's meant for me somehow. Even if I do get hurt in the end. I just want to be with her as much as I can.

I waited for Caroline's call the entire night when I got back to my dorm room, but it never came. The next night, I took the bus over to her place hoping to find her in. No one answered her buzzer. I went to a small bar down the block from where she lived and wrote her a long note. Why hadn't she called? Did I do something to make her mad at me? I didn't want to leave the note in the lobby of her apartment building, so I rang a bunch of the other buzzers in the building until I got someone to buzz me in. As I neared the door to Caroline's apartment, I heard loud music coming from inside. She had been there the whole time and ignored my buzzing. I banged on her door and asked her to let me in. A twenty-dollar bill came out from under the door. What did that mean? I knocked again.

Caroline slipped a note to me under the door. It said, "GO THE FUCK AWAY."

It felt as if someone had punched me in the gut. I knocked some more, but the music just got louder.

She's told you what she wants now. Can't you just leave it at that and accept that you are better off without her?

That can't be it. I deserve an explanation.

What if she's not able or willing to give you one?

I won't ever accept that.

I went back to Caroline's apartment the next day and rang her bell. There was no response, so I had someone else in the building buzz me in again. As I approached her door, I could hear her TV so I knew she was home. I rang the doorbell to her apartment and kicked at the door. "Caroline, please just come to the door and talk to me for one minute and then I'll leave you alone. Forever if you'd like." There was no response. I remembered the hole in her skylight so I ran up to the roof and pulled off the canvas cover, so I could speak to her without her neighbors hearing me.

"Please Caroline. Doesn't this seem stupid to you? If you will just talk to me, I promise I'll go away."

For the next three hours I alternated between ringing her doorbell and speaking to her through the skylight but got no response from her. I couldn't imagine what she was doing behind her closed door. Finally, after I had made myself thoroughly obnoxious, she came to the door.

She crashed her fist against the door and screamed, "Go away or I'm gonna kick the shit out of you!"

With Caroline's size, I didn't doubt that she probably could beat me up if she wanted to. But I was not ready to give up yet. I ran back to the roof and wrote a note saying, "I'LL BE BACK!" I folded it into a paper airplane and flew it through the hole in her skylight into her apartment.

Don't you find this all a little ridiculous?

I can't let her go without a fight, Ah Kung.

Is it truly worth the fight?

If she's going to be this dramatic, then I'm going to show her that I can match it.

I left her apartment without having any physical harm done to me. I knew in my heart that this would not be the end of it. A few days later, I sent her a letter telling her that she wouldn't be able to get rid of me until she gave me some sort of explanation. I promised her that I would continue to go by her apartment until she told me why she was acting this way. She owed me an answer as to what I had done to deserve this kind of treatment. If she really wanted me to leave her alone, I told her, she'd better answer me. Having written that, I planned to wait at least a week before I went back. But I was depressed. One night, three or four days later, I thought that, if I got really drunk with a couple of my friends, maybe I would be able to stop thinking about her. Before getting drunk, I made my friends promise that they wouldn't let me go over to Caroline's that night, no matter what. It was stupid to make them promise that. I should have known that getting drunk would only make me think about her more so that I would eventually end up at her place. After threatening to hurt one of my friends who valiantly tried to keep her promise, I escaped and hopped on a bus to the East Side, determined to see Caroline.

When I got to Caroline's, she buzzed me right up. The intoxication I felt from all the beer seemed to disappear almost immediately—I hadn't expected to get that far so easily. As she opened the door for me I asked her, "Can I have an explanation?"

"I'm just having my dinner," she said very calmly. "Is it okay if finish eating first?"

I sat down and waited. She ate slowly and when she was finished she told me, "You know I hate having to explain myself."

I asked her, "What, were you laughing at me behind your door all that time?"

"I wasn't laughing," she answered with a melancholy sigh. "After you left for home, I took heroin again and stayed high for the next three days. Afterwards I didn't want to see anyone—I didn't care who it was. But you kept coming by and then, well, you just started to annoy me."

"I know," I told her. "I was trying to."

"So… That's all."

> *You have her explanation. Why don't you keep your promise now and let her go?*
>
> *How can I when it's clear she's in so much pain?*
>
> *You're just asking for more punishment.*

She asked me to stay a while, drink some beer with her, and watch a movie on her new VCR. After all that had happened, it seemed strange to me for us to act like nothing had changed. But I wasn't about to complain—I had been hoping that we might get back together. Deep down, I knew that was what I had really come for. To stay overnight at her place right away, however, would have been pushing it, so at around three in the morning, I left for home. As I was leaving, Caroline said to me, "So, let's make plans and stick to them," as if it had been my fault that our plans hadn't materialized before. She told me that she had my number and would call me. I had heard that before but was willing to give her another chance to keep her word.

When she called me a few days later, I truly was pleasantly surprised. Not only that, she was calling from her own phone, which meant that I would no longer have to go all the way to her apartment when I wanted to get in touch with her. It seemed like a good sign. We made plans for me to go over to her place that Friday. On Thursday night, I called her to confirm that we were still on for the next evening, and she asked me if I wanted to meet her that night at the bar where we had first met. I couldn't refuse her.

When she arrived at the bar, about half an hour late, she seemed a bit wired and ordered two shots in quick succession. Caroline was determined to get drunk and all I could do was watch her do it. She ignored me most of the time we were there, then suddenly dragged me to another women's bar a few blocks away. The second bar was fairly crowded and, for some reason, Caroline and I seemed to attract a lot of attention. One older woman insisted upon announcing to the whole bar that she liked me.

"You're a good person," the woman asserted. "I'm a psychic, you know. And I can tell these things."

"And what about me?" Caroline asked her.

"You? You're bad."

"Ha ha ha."

"Are you two together?" she asked gesturing at Caroline and me. I looked at Caroline to see how she would react. I couldn't read her expression

Hesitantly I answered, "I guess so."

Then Caroline asked this woman who professed to have a sixth sense, "Hey, do you think I'm too old for her?"

"Not at all," the woman answered, looking towards me.

"Do you think I'm too old for her?" I joked.

"Definitely."

Caroline got bored with the place after a while and asked me to go back to her apartment with her. Willingly, I left with her, but I don't know why she wanted me with her that night. As soon as we got back to her apartment, she went straight for her kitchen cabinet and pulled out a hypodermic needle and a package of heroin. Ignoring me, she went into her bathroom to shoot up. I sat on her bed paralyzed with confusion and anguish.

Didn't I warn you this would happen?

Maybe I should try to grab the needle away from her.

I don't think so. She could try to hurt you.

She must have asked me to be with her tonight for a reason. Maybe she was hoping that I could stop her.

Maybe she wanted you to see who she really is. This may be her way of pushing you away without hurting your feelings.

More likely, it's that she's testing me to see if I will abandon her when she needs me most.

Can't you see it's useless? You are just a distraction, barely even background scenery in her drama.

But I wanted to save her from all this.

It was foolish to believe you could save her.

I thought I could do it by just loving her. I didn't think I'd have to watch her do all this.

You don't.

Caroline made a phone call after she returned from the bathroom. I couldn't hear all of it but, from what I could hear, it seemed that she was calling her dealer to get more heroin. She left the apartment without even acknowledging me.

At about five in the morning, I heard her come back, but I didn't want to open my eyes. I had gotten under the covers of her bed while she was out and continued to lie there pretending to be asleep. I heard her moving around the apartment, not knowing if she was shooting up again. Eventually, I really did fall asleep out of true exhaustion.

I awoke a few hours later to a kiss on my forehead. "Good morning, love." I opened my eyes to see her crouching beside me. The way she smiled when she looked at me made my heart melt.

"You know," she told me in a soft voice. "You really made me angry before, but I missed you. Move over, I want to get in."

She stripped down to her white cotton dress shirt and slipped into the bed beside me. Her long arms encircled me, and she entwined her legs with mine. Then she kissed me. It had been weeks since we had made love, and this felt so good. We stayed in bed together until the early afternoon.

It is worth it, Ah Kung. It really is.

Could this just be compulsion or obsession or even lust?

I'm not sure how I'm supposed to know. It doesn't just feel like obsession or lust to me. But I've never really felt like I loved anyone before. She can make me feel worse than anyone I've ever met. But when I feel like she loves me, it feels better than anything I've ever known.

Isn't she just lying to you now, though? She told you she used to be a junkie. But she's shown you she still is.

That's not her fault. I mean, that's what I'd like to make her understand— that she doesn't have to keep punishing herself for the unforgiveable things that have happened to her. She thinks the drugs help her forget. But they just make her feel worse about herself. Then she needs more of them to keep forgetting.

What makes you think you are an expert on drug abuse? Or any other kind of abuse?

I'm not. I just think she deserves compassion and help more than judgment and abandonment.

Maybe so. But why does it have to come from you?

*   *   *

It was a few days before Easter and Caroline agreed to meet my friend Jamie from school. Jamie was one my new gay friends and I was crazy for her, though not in a sexual way. I saw myself almost as a photographic negative image of her. We were alike, but opposites in a lot of ways. I had dark hair and darker skin while Jamie was blond and very pale. I was shy and Jamie was wild and outgoing. Jamie had had a lot of girlfriends since the middle of high school and Caroline was my first. I was excited for Jamie to meet Caroline and see what she thought.

We all got together at the Dublin House on Seventy-Ninth Street where Caroline and I had our first kiss. It was also on the same block where Jamie's off-campus housing was. We stood together around a small round bar table and drank and smoked cigarettes. Caroline and Jamie were both drinking highballs. I stuck with beer because I liked that I could regulate my drinking with it. I could always tell when I had just enough beer to feel loose and not get drunk or sick. I tried to read Jamie's face to see what she thought about Caroline, but she wasn't giving me any signals. The conversation, however, seemed to flow nicely.

"You're an introvert trying to get out," Caroline told me. She turned to Jamie. "And you're an extrovert trying to get in." We all laughed.

"Not bad," Jamie told me when Caroline left for the bathroom. I was bursting with pride.

At around seven thirty, we had to leave the bar and head up toward Eighty-Sixth Street where Jamie was scheduled to babysit. I was worried that she had had too much to drink to babysit, but Jamie didn't care. She bought a pack of gum at the Korean grocery store on the corner, while Caroline and I continued up Broadway holding hands. Suddenly someone was on Caroline's back pulling her down to the sidewalk. It was Jamie.

"What the fuck?" Caroline asked.

Jamie is just about my height and weighs less than me, and it wasn't difficult for Caroline to push her away and free herself from Jamie's wrestling hold. "You're fucking crazy."

Jamie just laughed. "Hey, I've got some weed. You want to smoke it with me before I go babysit?"

"Sure," Caroline answered

"I'll just keep lookout," I said.

We all sat by the bottom steps of a brownstone about ten houses away from Jamie's job that night. Caroline and Jamie shared a joint and I just smoked a cigarette. When they were finished smoking, Jamie took off and aired out her jacket, a long black trench coat, and popped in another piece of gum. She told us to wait around for about a half hour and come to the house where she was babysitting after the parents left. I wasn't sure it was such a good idea, but Caroline seemed to think it would be fun.

Caroline and I bought a large bottle of malt liquor and drank it out of a paper bag on the same brownstone steps where Caroline and Jamie smoked their pot. We waited a good forty-five minutes before going to the brownstone Jamie had disappeared into, just to be sure the parents were gone. Jamie let us into the large brownstone that was inhabited by that family alone, unlike the brownstone my brother lived in, which was a multi-tenant apartment building. There was a little blond toddler in a playpen in the living room. The place had wall-to-wall white carpeting, a fancy chandelier over the dining room table, and high-quality furniture all around. It was clear that the tenants of the house were rich. Jamie gave us a tour and introduced us to the toddler, who didn't seem to care who we were.

When we finished the tour, Jamie announced, "I feel like taking a shower. I love the way water feels when you're stoned."

Caroline exclaimed, "Me too. Let's." And before I could say anything, the two of them were racing up the stairs to the master bathroom.

What kind of friends are these?

I don't know. This isn't right. Caroline's supposed to be my girlfriend and Jamie is supposed to be one of my best friends. I don't know how they can do this to me. Maybe they both think I'm a big sucker who will just take it.

Isn't it time you got your self-respect back? What are you going to do?

I'm going to get out of here.

At last.

But I've got to go tell them I'm going.

Oh, Sya Meh. Why?

I walked upstairs to the master bedroom. I could hear Jamie and Caroline laughing in the shower. "Look, this is fucked," I called in to them, "so I'm going to take off."

"Wait," Caroline said. "I'm getting out right now. I'll leave with you."

"Okay. But it better be right now."

"Yes. Right now. I promise." I heard the water turn off.

"I'll be downstairs."

The toddler was holding onto and shaking the railing of her playpen and crying. I walked up to her and told her it was okay. She shook the railing more violently and screamed even louder and then fell on her backside. I picked the little girl up and rocked her. The tears were streaming down both our faces. I rocked her gently until we both stopped crying.

Caroline came barreling down the steps fully dressed, including her jacket. "Are you ready to go?" she asked.

"Yeah," I said, and tenderly placed the baby back in her playpen. She didn't cry when I sat her down in the pen. I patted her and gave her a little kiss on the top of her head, hoping that Jamie would regain her sense of responsibility to care for the little girl until her parents returned.

"I'd better get on home now," Caroline told me when we reached the street.

"Yeah, me too." I responded coolly. We walked together in silence to Broadway.

"Well, see you," I said when we reached the stairs to the subway.

"Okay, ciao."

On Sunday, I attended Easter service at the Riverside Church a few blocks up the street from Barnard. I hadn't been to a church since hearing a "Buddhists can't get into heaven" sermon delivered at my Presbyterian church back in Orange, New Jersey. At Riverside, I was so overtaken by the beauty of the cathedral, the music of the choir, and the incredible power of the compassionate and insightful sermon delivered by the senior minister that I was brought to tears three or four times during the service. This place was nothing like the church I had joined and then abandoned in my teenage years. It was completely racially integrated and had an incredible liberal quality. It occurred to me that, if I weren't gay and he were forty years younger, I might fall in love with the senior minister, the Reverend Dr. William Sloane Coffin. After the service, I stopped by the security desk where printed sermons of previous services were displayed and found a pamphlet on the Church's officially adopted statement of openness and inclusion of homosexuals. There was also a notice about the Riverside's gay and lesbian group called "Maranatha," which had been a secret greeting used by the early-persecuted Christians to identify each other.

This place blows me away. They might even let you and me into heaven here. I'm so glad I decided to come. I felt so close to God at times during the service.

Is that why you cried? Not because your friends hurt you?

Yeah they hurt me, but I don't think that was why I was crying. I'm not sure exactly why it moves me so, but this place truly makes me feel like I'm in God's presence. And somehow that touches me in a way I can't explain. They're tears of joy, I think. I feel very lucky to have found a place like this right now.

As I rounded the corner of 116th Street after the service, I ran into Jamie. "Where are you coming from all dressed in white?" she asked me.

"I was at Easter service at Riverside Church," pointing back to its beautiful tower.

"God, look at you all in white and I'm all in black. Now, what does that say about us?" she mused.

"I don't know," I said but I liked the symbolism.

She started rummaging in the pocket of her trench coat. "You know, I've been hoping to run into you because Caroline left her watch in the shower at my babysitting job. I got in a lot of trouble for it. Fired, you know. And the parents complained about me so I think I might get banned from Barnard babysitting."

I was glad of that. It served her right. "Thanks. I'll make sure Caroline gets it."

"Well…" she was struggling to come out with something to say and the expression on her face was pained.

"It's all right," I told her.

"Yeah? Really?"

"Sure, don't worry about it."

> *You really can forgive her?*
>
> *It's Easter, after all. Jesus is all about forgiveness.*
>
> > *Forgiveness, yes. But I don't think he wants you to be a "sucker," as you say.*
>
> *Well, I don't think forgiving her makes me a sucker.*
>
> > *What does it make you then?*
>
> *Maybe better than them.*

Caroline called me the next night. "You know that friend of yours is really crazy. Can you believe she jumped me right on the street?"

"No. But you must have liked it. Why else would you go and take a shower with her after that? Did you have sex with her in the shower?"

"Well, it was a sexual encounter. But, you know, we didn't have sex. It didn't really mean anything. I didn't mean anything by it. We were both just drunk and stoned, you know. I left with you, didn't I?"

"Never mind. So how are you doing?"

"Oh, I'm good. I think I have a way of making a lot of money."

"How?"

"There's this Muslim guy who knows a friend of mine. And he needs his papers. So he's willing to pay me $15,000 if I marry him."

"You'd really do that? That's crazy."

"No, it's easy. My friend did the same thing. You just have to stay married for a year or so and then you can get a divorce. It's no big deal."

The idea of Caroline getting married upset me. I felt my heart pounding, like I couldn't catch my breath. "But I don't want you to get married," I said, a little more forcefully than I intended.

"Now that's just silly. Anyway, it's not for sure. I'm still thinking about it. So anyway, we're still okay, right?"

"Yeah, we're okay," I told her.

"Good, let's get together later in the week and we can talk more about it."

*   *   *

My phone rang, waking me up. It was after three in the morning.

"Hey," Caroline said. "Do you mind if I ride my bike up to your place?"

"Now?"

"Yeah."

"I guess it'd be all right."

"Great, I'll be there in a jiff."

She seemed nervous and antsy when she got to my place. She was out of breath from riding across the park and the thirty blocks up from Eighty-Sixth Street. "Can I use your toothbrush?" she asked. "Where is it?" she probed when she saw that there were no toothbrushes in the bathroom. Because the six of us who lived in my off-campus housing suite shared a common bathroom, we all kept our toiletries in our own rooms.

I handed her a cup with my toothbrush and toothpaste. I watched her brush her teeth and then her tongue, which almost made her gag. She handed me back my things. "Do you want to?"

She had woken me up, so I figured I had a good case of morning breath. "Thanks," I said, and brushed my own teeth. While I was in the bathroom, Caroline had stripped naked and was waiting for me under the covers in my small twin-sized bed. I got into the bed on top of her with my clothes still on. Caroline undressed me under the covers and pressed herself against me, pulling me close as her pelvis met mine. "I love you," she breathed into my ear as she came.

We fell asleep together with me lying on top of her. It was the only way we fit in my single bed. When the sun rose, Caroline was stroking my hair. "I think I did something stupid last night," she said in a quiet, sad voice.

"What?" I asked.

"I don't know. Maybe something with dirty needles."

"What do you mean?"

"Never mind. It was just something stupid. Let's get some more sleep."

When we woke again, it was already the late afternoon and I had missed all my classes for that day. Caroline wanted to go back to her apartment since she had a bigger and more comfortable bed. I had been lying on her for hours and thought that her body was starting to feel too hot. We left her bike chained outside my building and took the bus to her place. For dinner, we got lasagna at a pizza place near her apartment and were both amused that anyone would make lasagna with English peas. Somehow we felt very close to each other because we both hated peas and meticulously picked them out from our dinner.

By around ten that night, Caroline was complaining of a headache and a sore back. She said she felt cold but, when I felt her forehead, she was burning up. We went to bed early and she shivered through the night. I held her tight and imagined that I could keep away all the bad things in her life. In the morning, I found her sleeping on her back with her calves resting on an upright chair on the bed. We laughed about how crazy it looked, but Caroline said it was the only way she could make her back feel better. She still felt warm to me, but she took some aspirin and said her headache wasn't as bad. I had to show up for my classes that day but promised to call later and come by to see how she was doing.

After my classes I called and there was no answer. I kept calling every half hour until well past midnight, but nobody picked up.

I just can't understand why this keeps happening.

Could it be that you keep letting it happen?

How am I letting it happen?

As long as she is a drug addict, and you still want to be with her while she's that way, won't this keep happening?

If I could just get her off the drugs.

When I called her the next morning, Caroline answered the phone. She confessed that she had gone out the night before to get high. She said she was in a lot of pain and that the drugs took the edge off. "I'm really sick now, though. I think my fever's real bad and there's something wrong with my hip. It hurts like hell."

"Let me come over and take care of you."

"Nah, Bill's coming over. I don't need you to come."

"I'm coming anyway," I said and hung up the phone before she could stop me.

When she let me in I saw she was crying. "It really hurts. I don't know what's wrong with me."

"Let me help you," I pleaded.

"No, you've got to go. Bill's already on his way and he's going to take me to a doctor or something. I really don't need or want you to be here."

"I don't understand this, Caroline. How can you be so hot and cold with me like this? If you were already sick, why would you go out last night?"

"Look, you're not my keeper. I'm free to do what I like. I don't have to answer to you." She was moving toward me, and it clearly hurt her to move. "Just get out, all right? I don't want to have to hurt you."

"What the hell are you talking about? You're going to hurt me if I don't get out?"

"No, I don't want to hurt you. I just want you to leave."

"I won't. You have to let me help you," I pleaded.

"God damn it. I want you out." She had made her way over to me and grabbed my knapsack and pulled it off my shoulder. Then she leaned against me and grabbed my leather jacket by the collar. Awkwardly she used her other hand to loosen the jacket from my shoulders and arms. I didn't know what she was doing and didn't fight her. "What are you doing?" I asked.

She took the jacket and grabbed up my bag and made her way to the window, hobbling in obvious pain. "If you won't leave on your own, then maybe you'll follow your things." She opened the window and dropped both my bag and leather jacket four stories down onto the sidewalk. "You'd better go get them before someone steals them," she announced.

I thought about it for a moment and decided that I did not want my jacket, an expensive gift from my parents, and my bag with all my schoolbooks and homework stolen.

"Fine, Caroline," I cried. "Live your life the way you want. I'm not gonna try to help you anymore."

"I never asked you to help me," she said in a voice that now sounded gentle and relieved.

But her gentleness wasn't going to win me back this time. I had already made up my mind and left the apartment. On my way down the stairs, I met Bill on his way up. I told him, "You take care of her. I'm done now."

I didn't wait for his response as I rushed to collect my things from the street.

Finally. You needed to let her go.

Maybe. But I wish it felt better.

CHAPTER 9
A STROKE OF
BAD LUCK

Matt was one of only two men that I had slept with more than once. I met him freshman year when he was the manager of a neighborhood bar that was a popular hangout for university students because they didn't check ID. He liked to think of himself as more of an actor than a bar manager, though his only real acting experiences were a small but memorable role in a John Waters movie and a brief appearance in the movie *Diner*—both shot in his home town of Baltimore. Since moving to New York, he was only able to get work in bars and had worked his way up to manager. He was handsome with a bit of a James Dean quality (though less distinctive), and the sex I had with him hadn't been all that bad. He and another bartender from the place he managed saved enough money to buy another tavern in the neighborhood on Amsterdam and 106th Street, so my friends and I started to hang out at Matt's new bar. It was dingy and catered to a drug-taking clientele (it sported an upstairs bathroom where people would go to snort cocaine), but it had a pool table that always featured lively competition. I had challenged Matt and beat him in two straight games of pool in front of a Friday night crowd and he walked away mad. He and I were just friends now, since I had told him I was gay, but when he left the table, it reminded me of how my first boyfriend in eighth grade broke up with me after I showed him up in a boys vs. girls snowball fight at ski camp. I had gone to the bar alone to celebrate finishing my final exams. Since Matt was my only friend there that night, the fact that he was mad at me made me feel sorry for myself in my inebriated state. I took my beer over to the payphone and dialed Caroline's number.

The voice that answered wasn't Caroline's.

"May I speak with Caroline, please?" I asked.

"Who is this?" the strange raspy voice asked.

"I'm a friend."

"A druggie friend?" she asked pointedly.

"No, I go to school up at Columbia University. We met a couple of months ago."

"Well, this is Caroline's mother and I'm sorry to have to tell you that Caroline's had a massive stroke. She just recently came out of a coma and we don't know the extent of her brain damage. We're not even sure she'll survive with all that she's suffered. She definitely has some paralysis and right now she can't speak at all."

"Oh my God." My heart started pounding. I wasn't sure I was still breathing. "She's in the hospital?" I asked weakly.

"Yes. Lenox Hill Hospital. But she's in critical condition still and she's not allowed visitors. You can keep calling the hospital. If her condition improves to something better than critical, they may let you visit her. I'm sorry but that's the best I can tell you. Thank you for calling." And with that she hung up.

I was shaking. I left the bar without saying anything to Matt and ran all the way back to my apartment on 110th Street.

How could this have happened, Ah Kung?

Are you really surprised by it, Sya Meh? You knew she was playing a dangerous game. Wasn't this an outcome you could have expected?

— 130 —

I never really believed that something so terrible would happen.

If you knew, would you have done anything differently?

Of course. I could have tried harder to save her. Maybe if I hadn't left her that afternoon, she wouldn't have had the stroke.

You tried as hard as you could.

Maybe if I didn't care so much about getting my own feelings hurt. I shouldn't have given up on her.

She gave up on you. Isn't she the one who threw you out?

I should have known better. I should have fought harder.

Why believe you can help someone who didn't want to be helped? It may make you feel better to think that you had some power over it, but your friend was the only one who had any control over her life.

I moved in with my brother for the summer while I worked as an intern at a large Wall Street investment company. The apartment was small—a one bedroom third floor walk-up in a brownstone on West Sixty-Ninth Street near Columbus Avenue. The door to the apartment opened into a small dining area with a kitchenette and tiny bathroom to the right. Around the door were built-in bookshelves filled with my brother's diverse book collection. From the dining area, you descended three short steps to the rest of the apartment that consisted of a living room and bedroom off to the right that only had room for a twin-sized bed and dresser and desk. It was a quaint apartment with brick lining most of the west wall in the living room/dining room and the east wall of the bedroom. Two African masks hung from the brick and an old red and black Oriental carpet cushioned the hardwood floor of the living room. The couch was a flimsy white-painted wood frame with a thin foam cushion upholstered with a zebra-like white and black fabric on the base and another cushion that folded for the back. The frame expanded and both cushions could be laid flat to make into my bed at night.

For weeks, I called the hospital every day to check on Caroline's condition. They always told me that her condition was critical. Then one Saturday, they told me her condition had changed to stable. I thought it might be a mistake.

"Are you sure?" I asked the receptionist.

"All I can tell you is that's what it says in the computer."

"And she can have visitors now?"

"She's in the ICU but, as far as I know, she can."

"Thanks very much." I ran outside to catch a crosstown bus to the hospital.

Are you sure you want to see her in this condition?

No. But I have to go.

Why do you have to? What do you expect to accomplish?

I just want to let her know that I'm sorry this happened to her. And that I still care about her and hope she gets better.

But why you? Why do you feel that you have a responsibility to her at all? She didn't even want you around in the end.

I can't explain it, but I feel that I'm meant to be in her life. I don't think I would feel this way about her if I wasn't meant to be a part of her life. I just don't think God would be random in that way.

What does God have to do with it? If God were involved, why wouldn't he just cure your friend of her drug addiction? Or better yet, why didn't he keep her from being molested as a child?

All I can tell you is that I feel that God has a plan for me and that I believe it involves Caroline somehow.

Is God's plan for everyone, or just you?

I don't know about everyone. But I definitely feel like He or She has a plan for me.

He or She. Why do people refer to God that way these days?

Because nobody really knows if God is male or female or both. It's more politically correct that way.

What will you do next to be politically correct? Call it the hu-person race instead of the human race?

Please take it easy on me! I need to gather my strength to see Caroline.

How do you propose to do that?

I'm going to pray.

Well, I hope He or She answers you.

Caroline's ICU room was private and the heavy wooden door at its entry had a window with diamond-patterned green wire running through it. I peeked in to see if anyone else was in the room with Caroline. She was alone, so I opened the door and went in. The fact that her hair was no longer blond surprised me, though I probably should have figured out earlier that nobody naturally has hair that light. And I wasn't used to seeing her wear her John Lennon-style glasses instead of contacts. Her light brown hair was shorter and straighter than when I had last seen her, and there was a prominent bald spot just above her right ear where there was a healing abrasion. It seemed that she recognized me, but her face wore a look of regret and heartache. Her eyes followed me as I made my way closer to her. Her mouth opened and closed as if trying to talk, but no sound escaped.

"Is it ok if I hold your hand?" I asked.

She nodded and moved her left hand to rest on the bed guardrail. Her right hand lay motionless and contorted by her right hip. I took her left hand in mine and gently squeezed it.

"Caroline, I am so sorry this happened to you."

Tears started to form in her eyes and she nodded rapidly and made quick gasps for air. She squeezed my hand back.

A nurse in pink scrubs came into the room. "Oh, she's not talking yet, but doing much better today, right dear?"

Caroline nodded some more. She looked at me pleadingly, but I didn't know what she was asking for. She moved my hand to her lips and kissed it with her soft, dry, cracking lips.

"It's fine," I told her. "We're going to get through all this."

"Her parents should be in soon," the nurse told me. She gathered the food tray that looked like it hadn't been touched. "If you wait awhile you can talk to them."

"No, that's ok. I just wanted to stop by and say hello to Caroline. I can't stay long."

I kissed Caroline on the forehead and told her I would stop by again the next day. She smiled and I felt her eyes follow me as I made my way to the door.

"I love you," I told her just before the door closed behind me. "See you tomorrow."

Do you really love her, Sya Meh?

I think I do.

Are you sure it's not just guilt or the fact that you feel sorry for her after what has happened?

Obviously, I feel bad for her. I always have because I don't think anyone should have had to go through what she did as a child. Somebody should have protected her from her brother. And now she's hurt herself more than anyone else could have. But that's why I love her—I see something in her that gets to me. She fights herself from being the loving and trusting person she could be. But she's never really had a reason to trust anyone.

She didn't just hurt herself. She hurt you too.

In comparison, it was nothing. Like you said, she was trying to protect me from her. But I think deep down she knew that I was someone good for her. So she couldn't quite push me away completely.

Is that love though? For either of you?

I just know that I still want to be a part of her life. I can't help admiring her for the fight that I see is in her—that has allowed her to make it this far after such a catastrophic event. I have to believe she's going to come out of it somehow.

Maybe. But what she will come out of it as?

*   *   *

I went to church the next day at Riverside and prayed to God for guidance. I didn't feel like I got a direct reply, but everything about the service moved me. Once again, the music of the interracial choir was incredible. There was even a musical interlude of Riverside's Rockefeller Memorial Carillon, an instrument with seventy-four bronze bells ranging in weight from twenty tons to ten pounds. Dr. Coffin's sermon was both moving and brilliant. He preached about homophobia. He said that the problem for Christians shouldn't be about reconciling homosexuality with otherwise discarded, obscure scriptural passages that condemn it. Rather, the problem for Christians is how to reconcile the rejection and punishment of homosexuals with the love of Christ. He insisted, "It can't be done." He preached that we should stop talking about what is natural and instead talk about what is normal, which for Christians should always be love, never condemnation or rejection. At the end of the sermon, he announced the formation of the parade and float committee for Riverside's participation in the Gay Pride Parade the next month and urged Riverside's members to sign up to represent the church in the parade. I was moved to tears again, hearing the beautiful harmonies of the choir's "Amen," which echoed from the vestibule at the entrance of the main worship space of the Cathedral following Dr. Coffin's benediction. What a different kind of church this was. It filled me with love, hope, and strength for my next visit with Caroline.

*　　　　*　　　　*

Caroline was alone in her ICU room except for the nurse changing her bed sheets. I asked if it was okay to come in and the nurse said sure. Caroline smiled when she saw me. The nurse had to roll Caroline on her side to remove the old sheet and slide the new sheet into place. I looked away so as not to stare at Caroline's exposed back and bottom from her hospital gown. The nurse rolled Caroline back toward me to remove and replace the other side and Caroline laughed as she looked at me. I was impressed at how expertly the nurse performed her work to change the sheets with Caroline still on the bed. She did it all with a gentleness and good humor that seemed to please Caroline. Then she floated a clean top sheet over Caroline and added a thin, clean cotton blanket over the top. When she was done, she gently patted Caroline on the shoulder and said, "Otay Panky, all done."

Caroline opened her mouth and breathed out. Softly, slowly, and in a lower tenor than before her stroke, she replied, "Otay Buckwheat," and laughed.

"Huh? Are those the first words she's spoken?" the nurse asked me.

"I don't know. This is only the second time I've come to visit her. But I don't think she was talking yesterday."

Caroline laughed again, a little more loudly. She looked at me and motioned with her left hand for me to come closer. When I leaned down close to her lips, she spoke very slowly in low voice.

"I love you. You're a good person and I'm supposed to love you."

"I love you too," I told her as tears welled up in my eyes.

She turned to the nurse. "I love you too."

Chapter 10

SILENCE = DEATH

Caroline's parents picked me up at the Will Rogers Oklahoma City airport in a two-toned brown, wood-paneled Jeep wagon and drove me to their home. The property was on a large acre-and-a-quarter lot and included a massive two-story shop for her father's air conditioning business as well as multiple outbuildings, including an old horse barn. While the cigar-stenched and messy office was the domain of Caroline's pack rat father, Caroline's mother kept the rest of the home in an immaculate state, with every tacky knickknack proudly on display. Her mother's surprisingly high-quality original paintings lined practically every wall in the home, with the exception of Caroline's seventh grade charcoal drawing of three Native Americans that had won an honorable mention award and now hung on wood paneling above the couch in the den.

As she added sheets and a blanket to this couch for my stay, Caroline's mother told me that Caroline had AIDS. It seemed that the dirty needle that led to Caroline's stroke also was infected with the virus that caused AIDS. There was something apologetic or pitiful in her tone as she told me. It was as if she was saying, "If you were thinking about having a life with Caroline, I'm sorry, but you're barking up the wrong tree." Caroline was being kicked out of the rehab hospital to an AIDS residence. In 1986, nobody in Oklahoma knew much about AIDS, even in the medical community, and their fear of it overpowered any desire they might have had to help Caroline recover from her stroke. Besides, they believed AIDS was a death sentence, so why bother with physical therapy?

It's not fair, Ah Kung. Why would God save her from dying from a stoke only to kill her with AIDS?

Why think God has anything to do with it?

Because God has something to do with everything. Even the doctors at Lenox Hill thought it was a miracle that Caroline survived. She wasn't even found for two days after her stroke. She has to have lived because God felt that she had more to do.

What more do you think she has to do?

I don't know yet. That's between her and God.

But if she has AIDS now…

No! I won't believe that God has changed his mind!

I surprised Caroline in the therapy room at the O'Donoghue Rehabilitation Institute. She had lost a lot of the weight from the time she was on steroids. Her hair had been badly cut by a beauty school student and no longer had any traces of the blond color I had so admired when we met. The jeans she wore looked like they had been her mother's, cut way too high in the waist and far too wide in the legs. Her sneakers were a dull white with wide Velcro straps in place of laces, and she had on a white T-shirt from a Mexican bar and restaurant with three frogs sporting the see no evil, hear no evil and speak no evil poses. She was sitting with her mother in her wheelchair when I entered the room. A big smile came over her face when she saw me.

"They said I have AIDS and I'm gonna die."

"Hush up, Caroline. Everyone doesn't need to know our business," Caroline's mother scolded, looking around.

"I'm happy to see you," she told me.

"I'm happy to see you too," I told her and gave her a hug.

"I have to do my therapy now. But you can stay and watch."

"Thanks, I'd like that."

"I can't really walk yet."

"Yes, you can," Caroline's mother insisted. "You just have to work harder."

"I'm trying, mother."

"Trying is a cop-out."

The therapy session was grueling. The stretching of her atrophied right arm and leg looked painful and I could see tears in Caroline's eyes as they manipulated her stiff limbs. She verbalized, "Some kind of stretch," and even "That's too much" several times. But the therapist continued the stretches no matter what Caroline said. After the stretching, they brought Caroline to a ramp with rails on both sides and pulled her up to a standing position. They had her grab the rail to her left to traverse the ramp. Caroline had exaggerated her inability to walk. She was able to drag herself back and forth across the ramp four times. While her right leg didn't exactly make a normal stride, she was able to swing it around in front of her and hold up her body weight by holding the rail with her good hand.

After her walking exercise, she plopped back down into her wheelchair exhausted. I followed behind her as they wheeled her back to her room. Once she was back in the bed in her small private room, her mother left us alone for a while to talk.

"I'm scared," she told me. "I don't want to die."

"You're not going to die."

"But they told me I am. I have to move to an AIDS hospice next week. I wanted to move back home, but my mother told me I can't. I have to do things by the book now and live with other people with AIDS."

"I'm sorry. That doesn't seem right. But maybe it's a nice place."

"Where do you think you go when you die?"

"I'm not sure. But I don't think dying is the end of everything. I think there's something else, whether it's heaven or being born to another life."

"I had other lives before."

"Really?"

"One time, I think I was a black slave and Janie was my black baby."

"You mean your best friend, Janie?"

"Yeah, that's why we bonded so quickly when we met in grade school. And another time, I think I was a vagabond in England. And once I was a prostitute named Annabel. I've had a lot of interesting past lives. But I'm still afraid of dying."

I should be better at this. I mean, I have faith and believe in God and some kind of afterlife. Maybe even in reincarnation like Buddhists and Caroline. But I don't know how to share my beliefs with her in a way that comforts her at all.

You're doing fine.

And how could I tell her she isn't going to die? I can't know that.

She won't hold it against you.

I can't imagine that Dr. Coffin would have any problem comforting someone in Caroline's position.

Why be so hard on yourself? This is all new to you. You just found a faith that speaks to you and now you learn that Caroline is dying. It's a lot to expect of yourself.

I admire Dr. Coffin so much, I really think I can imagine myself becoming a minister if I could handle conversations like this a little better.

It's a worthy occupation, no doubt. But is your faith that important to you?

I guess all this will help me find out.

Before the end of my three-day visit with Caroline, her parents let her come home to spend one night while I was there. When they told me it would be all right for me to stay in Caroline's room even though there was only one full-sized bed in it, I wondered if her parents understood the nature of my relationship with Caroline or if they just thought two girlfriends sharing a bed was innocent enough. Between us, there were no thoughts of making love while we shared the bed. But I considered it a wonderful, tender gift to have a chance to feel the warmth of Caroline's body against mine one more time. She held me close through the night and whispered to me before we fell asleep, "Someday we'll be together again."

I knew I would find a way to visit again very soon.

Just over a month later, a few days after Christmas, I fought with my parents about Caroline. I told them that I was going to spend what I could of the Christmas break from school visiting Caroline. I couldn't afford the airfare, so I had bought a ticket on a Trailways bus from New York to Oklahoma City—a thirty-six-hour trip.

My mother avoided conversations with me about Caroline. She knew I had seen Caroline in the hospital throughout the summer. But I was staying with my brother then, so my mother had no say in how I spent my free time. When I told her I was gay two years earlier, she wouldn't talk to me about it. But I would catch her walking through the house in her nightgown crying. When I tried to ask what was wrong, she refused to discuss it with me. I imagined my relationship with Caroline was even harder for my mother to take. It meant that being gay wasn't just a phase for me. And nobody could ignore the complications that a relationship with Caroline now presented. But I was already committed and I dug in.

"How can you waste your life caring about someone like that?"

"You don't know anything about her," I told her. "You don't know what she's been through."

"I don't care. She is not my daughter. I care about what you do with your life."

"Well it's my life."

"Not while you are under my roof."

"Then I don't need to be under your roof."

I packed up, took a train into New York, and hopped on the bus four days earlier than I had originally planned. *Fear and Trembling*, the classic book on faith by the nineteenth century Danish philosopher and theologian Søren Kierkegaard, kept me company. All those hours on the bus to Oklahoma City gave me a lot of time to wonder if I had left my parents' house for the last time. It was my father's roof too and he had told me before that he would always love and support me no matter what. My mother, on the other hand, had used the "not under my roof" line before. But this was the first time I actually left the house and went somewhere far from them. It wasn't that I worried about losing funding for my last semester of college. They had already paid for that and I figured they would be too proud to ask for it back. But I wasn't sure if I was really ready to live without the emotional support of my parents.

At a rest stop in Indiana I bought a gold-colored ring with a moderately sized cubic zirconia stone.

Your mother is just trying to protect you. And she may not be wrong.

She has no right to tell me what to do or how to feel. I can't help being in love with Caroline, no matter what's happened to her.

What does the ring mean?

I don't know if I'll give it to her. But I want her to know I still love her and I can see myself spending my life with her.

Won't your life be much longer than hers?

Her life with me then.

Caroline had been living in an AIDS residence called The Winds for a couple of weeks. When she greeted me, she sang off-tune "all we are is dust in The Winds." There were three other residents, all gay men in their 20s, and a middle-aged house manager. The home was also where all the other men with AIDS in Oklahoma City would come to visit friends and get support. I was particularly struck by a beautiful young man named Blake who came to visit Ken, the house manager. Blake was about six feet tall, with straight blond hair, piercing blue eyes, and a perfect smile.

"Hi gorgeous," he called out to Caroline. "Who's your friend?"

She introduced me as her friend from New York.

"I've always wanted to go to New York. Not sure if I'll ever make it there now."

Caroline maneuvered herself around the house in a wheelchair, using her one good arm and one good leg. She was no longer getting any physical therapy.

"Blake is such a dear heart," she told me. "He's talked about wanting to plan his funeral now while he's still healthy. He wants it to be a wonderful celebration of his life, with lots of laughing and singing. He says he's going to treat us to cases of high-end champagne. Blake was going to college, but now he's dedicating the rest of his life to AIDS advocacy."

It's so heartbreaking, Ah Kung. To see all these young people here. They should have their whole lives ahead of them, but instead they're contemplating the end of their lives.

Many of your faith feel differently. Don't they blame these young people for their own demise?

That's nothing but an ugly distortion of Christianity. They want to blame people who have AIDS, saying that it's God's punishment for the sins they committed. But I heard Dr. Coffin give another amazing sermon on AIDS based on a New Testament reading from the Gospel of John about a man born blind. The disciples asked Jesus who had sinned, the man's parents or him, that he was born blind. And Jesus answered that neither sinned. He told the disciples that the man was born blind so that God's love could be revealed through him. Then Jesus healed the blind man. Dr. Coffin preached that AIDS is not God's punishment for sin but rather our opportunity to demonstrate God's love by ministering to the sick.

Is it your opportunity?

I'd like to care for her any way I can.

You're sure you want to keep Caroline in your life?

Yes. If she'll have me.

With Caroline lying in bed in the small first floor bedroom at The Winds, we talked about how she saw her future.

"I tested positive for *Cryptosporidium*. I'm not supposed to have much time left."

"I don't know what that is."

"It's some kind of parasite."

"I've never heard of it. I thought people who have AIDS get pneumonia or skin cancer. Are you sure it has to do with AIDS?"

"The doctor's sure. He says that it's easy for anyone to get *Cryptosporidium*, like from regular tap water. But if you don't have AIDS, you can get rid of it. Since I have the parasite and I've been throwing up all the time, they say I may only have a few months to live. Can you help me put a pillow under my knees? It helps my backache."

She had four pillows behind her head, since it was just a normal flat bed. I helped her lean forward so I could slip out one of the pillows. She was able to bend her left knee, but needed my support to lift her right one. I put my hand gently on her leg, then slid it over to her left hand and squeezed it. Tears started to form in Caroline's eyes.

"My daddy says big girls don't cry."

"You have every right to cry." I gently massaged her hand.

"I thought I'd have time to make things right. But now I have to make plans like Blake."

"I don't want you to give up." I pulled out the ring I bought at the Indiana rest stop. "I want you to have this. Can I put it on you?" I asked bringing her hand closer to me.

Caroline looked at the ring and saw immediately that it was far too small to fit on her ring finger.

"Maybe on this," she laughed as she extended her pinky. "That way it won't mean too much." It was a little tight on her pinky and even for a fake diamond it looked pathetically small on Caroline's large hand. She ran her fingers through my hair and patted my head playfully.

"Thank you anyway," she added. "It's nice that you came to see me again. But I think you should go home now."

"I was planning to stay for my whole break. Your parents don't seem to mind my staying with them longer."

"It's not for them. It's for you. You're getting too attached. It's not good for you. You've got your life to live and I've got plans to make. We can still write each other and talk sometimes on the phone. We'll keep in touch, okay?"

I can't believe she's making me leave, when she's so sad and alone. I hate that she's pushing me away when she needs me most.

It seems that she's being quite kind.

But I don't need her to protect me any more than I need my mother to. I really believed we were meant to be together.

How do you see that happening?

It can happen if I make a leap of faith like Abraham or the Knight of Faith from Kierkegaard's "Fear and Trembling."

Is your faith that strong?

Well I don't really believe that Abraham was one hundred and Sarah ninety when Isaac was born. Plus, it's a pretty gruesome story to have God demand Isaac's sacrifice after giving him a son at the age of one hundred. It's clearly meant to be an important allegory on faith.

How does faith relate to love?

That's what the Knight of Faith was all about. I don't know how many times I had to read that part of the book over and over to try to get my mind around it. It was about how resignation—which, according to Kierkegaard, doesn't mean giving up your heart's desire—is what leads to faith. He wrote, "Infinite resignation is the last stage before faith, so anyone who has not made this movement does not have faith."[1] I couldn't get my mind around it and it made my head hurt. I guess that's what faith is, though. If Kierkegaard is right, maybe the only way that

---

[1]   Søren Kierkegaard, Fear and Trembling (London: Penguin Books Ltd, 1985), 46.

Caroline and I can be together is if I resign myself to the impossibility of it.

When I boarded the bus in Oklahoma City for the trip back to New York, I was one of only three passengers. I took the last seat in the back, closest to the bathroom in the smoking section. We passed through all the same "heartland of America" cities I had seen for the first time on my way to see Caroline, in backward order: Tulsa, St. Louis, Indianapolis, Columbus, Pittsburgh. At the final three stops, beginning with Philadelphia, we took on several dozen passengers, filling every seat by the time we reached Grand Central Station. I took a deep breath and held it in as we slowly ascended the ramps of the last two stories of the bus terminal. When the bus came to a stop, I let my breath out. After thirty-six hours, the last four minutes waiting for all the other passengers to disembark felt like an eternity.

When I finally felt the concrete floor of the terminal under my feet and got my things from the luggage compartment, I was elated. But then I realized I wasn't sure where I should go. There were still four days before my final college term would start. Should I go back home to spend those days with my parents in New Jersey? I wasn't sure of my welcome.

Why not call your parents? They would want to know you're safe.

I feel that would be groveling. I'm not going to apologize for wanting to spend time with Caroline.

Is it so hard to apologize? Or is it that you don't want to admit your mother was right about things not working out with Caroline?

Caroline has more important things to worry about than hurting me. I'm a big girl. I can take care of myself.

But you don't have to.

I feel like I should try

I headed to the dorm. My private bedroom in apartment 8-P of the College Residence Hotel was unbelievably large for student housing. I shared the apartment with two sophomores who both stayed in what would have been a living room/dining room in a normal one-bedroom apartment. I got the huge bedroom with a queen-sized bed (probably the only one in all of student housing), while the sophomores shared the common space between my bedroom and the kitchen. The residence hall began its life as a pre-World War II New York apartment building, and students still shared about a third of the building with other neighborhood residents. The apartment had well-worn red and black carpeting throughout, thick walls that had been covered over dozens of times with high-gloss white paint, old electrical outlets of dubious safety, a simple four-piece bathroom with fixtures from the 1950s, and a large eat-in kitchen. Since my apartment-mates were still home for Christmas break, I had the whole place to myself.

On the way to Oklahoma, all I had to eat was hastily purchased fast food from rest stops, then nothing but beef and potatoes in Oklahoma City, and more fast food on the trip back. Back in my own space, I fixed myself dinner of ramen noodles with a scrambled egg and Chinese cabbage from the Korean grocer around the corner. It was comforting to eat Asian food, even if only made from a dry packet. I ate it sitting at the kitchen table right from the pot with chopsticks and a white plastic Chinese soupspoon. After I finished my dinner, I walked the eight blocks up to campus to see if I had received any mail at the student mail room.

When I saw the envelope postmarked from Brazil, I struggled to imagine why anyone from there would write me. Then I remembered my letter. I had gone to see a lecture by one of my anthropology professors where he shared video footage of supposed healings performed by a Brazilian faith-healing "doctor" named John of God. Among other examples, the video showed him using nothing but his fingers to remove a grapefruit-sized tumor out of an inch-wide incision from a woman with breast cancer. After the lecture, I approached my professor.

"I'm not sure if this is appropriate to ask, but do you believe the doctor was actually performing faith-healing miracles?"

"It's okay to ask. Well, let me put it this way. There were many things I witnessed firsthand that I couldn't just explain away as trickery."

"There were no tricks?"

"Well, I wouldn't say that. A magician friend of mine analyzed my footage and he was convinced that the doctor had hypnotized not just the patients he operated on but also the entire audience. He also thought it was highly likely that the doctor was using things like chicken livers to represent the tumors and other ailments he was removing in his surgeries. But the incisions themselves appeared real."

"Then what were the things you couldn't explain?" I pressed him.

"The woman from the breast cancer operation, for example. I personally accompanied that woman when she got a CAT scan that showed widespread metastases from her breast cancer before the faith healing operation. And three months after she was operated on by the faith healer, I went with her to get a new CAT scan. It no longer showed any metastases or tumors in her breasts. Now, more than a year later, she still seems to be in complete remission."

"But if the healings were real, why would he have to use chicken livers?"

"That's the interesting thing," he mused. "The faith healer told me his operations are only for show because so many people do not have enough faith to heal themselves without a physical intervention. He claims he can heal people just as successfully at a distance, with no operation at all. For the truly faithful, he said, he can heal just by sending a letter."

"How would that work?"

"I think you just write the doctor and he sends instructions."

"Do you have his address?"

"Stop by during my office hours tomorrow and I'll give it to you."

I had written to the faith healer requesting his help to perform a faith healing "surgery" at a distance for Caroline, even before I learned she had Cryptosporidium and her doctor gave her only a few months to live. I felt my heart beating powerfully through my chest as I opened the envelope with the Brazilian postmark. My eyes filled with tears when I discovered that the letter from him was completely in Portuguese.

I paced around the mailroom in a panic, forcing my breath out through pursed lips trying to figure out what to do. Were there any Portuguese language professors at Columbia who might be around during the winter break? The campus was nearly deserted, other than the occasional security personnel who would smile and wave at me when I passed by. It was doubtful that I would be able to find anyone who read Portuguese this week. Was the library open? I prayed that it would be open during the winter break, even though, intellectually, I knew that if the library was closed, my prayers couldn't magically open it.

I was breathing heavily with clouds of cool vapor forming when I put my hand on the heavy, ornate doors to Butler Library. I pulled on the handle.

"Thank you, God," I said as the door swung open.

"Studying during the winter break, honey?" the female security guard asked me when I showed her my ID.

"Yes," I lied. The true explanation would have sounded crazy.

"It's pretty empty here today. You're not planning to go up to the stacks, are you? It might get kinda scary up there all on your own."

"No, I only need to go to the reference room today." She was right about the scary stacks. The lights there were on timers, and if you couldn't find your book quickly enough, you would find yourself fumbling in the dark to find the light switch again. But when school was in session, you could at least hear other people rustling around in a nearby aisle. Wandering around the stacks when I was the only person in the whole library would really be foreboding.

It wasn't too hard to find a Portuguese to English dictionary in the reference room. Trying to translate the doctor's letter into English was another story. It took me two hours, and I wasn't confident I got everything right.

Recommendations for Liquid Therapy at a Distance:

During the week before:

Attend doctrinal meetings

Read evangelical messages

Pray, think vigilantly, and

Avoid major physical exertion

On the day of treatment, January 13, 1987,

Keep conversations and vibrations positive from the time of daybreak

Don't smoke or drink alcohol

Make nourishment mild, without flesh (meat?), crustaceans, preserves, fat, fried things, fruit acids, chocolate, coconut, etc.

Make your last meal really early

At 7:30 p.m. collect yourself at your bed, in partial shadows (candlelight?), wear white clothes, in order to meditate about Jesus while you sleep

Place a cup of water at your head, to take at 11:00 p.m. or when you wake

The period of recovery:

At 12:00 a.m. following surgery, keep yourself in bed with temperate nourishment

On the following Thursday or Friday, continue the same diet, including the other days, marked with spiritual visions

Avoid running for eight days totally

Thank God for the blessings received, which should always be proportional to their worth

It was already less than a week before the scheduled "surgery." I hadn't been exerting myself physically but had I prayed enough, read enough evangelical messages, and could I attend enough doctrinal meetings before Tuesday? How would this work, anyway? Could I follow the instructions but still have Caroline be the one that gets healed?

I walked the five blocks to Riverside Church and prayed in the meditation chapel, an intimate space around the corner from the main chancel. That prayer was one of dozens of prayers I said that week. On Sunday, I went to Riverside to hear Dr. Coffin preach on "The Beginning."[2] Once again, it was a brilliant and challenging sermon about Genesis and how we should approach Genesis as intellectually curious, progressive Christians.

Are you more interested in the process of creation or in the purpose of creation?

---

[2] William Sloane Coffin, "The Beginning, January 11, 1987" in *Collected Sermons of William Sloane Coffin, The Riverside Years*, vol. 2 (Louisville: Westminster John Knox Press, 2008).

Whether the earth took billions of years to come into being or was made in six days in no way affects the central truth of creation, which is that the universe did not come to be by chance. It is God who made us and the world we live in. This we know not by science, nor by cold reason, which can defend the existence of God but never discover it. This we know by what God has put into the human heart, by what our spirits tell us: namely, that human beings are made for someone grander than themselves.

To insist on a literal interpretation of the creation stories in Genesis is to confuse the "how" and the "why" questions, to confuse facts and meaning (once all the facts are in, no one has the truth!); it is to pit science against religion, misunderstanding the intentions of both.

He quoted Tolstoy (a favorite author of mine), who said, "Certain questions are put to us not so much that we should answer them, but that we should spend a lifetime wrestling with them."

And while Dr. Coffin said he would leave the beginning of sin for his sermon the following week, he said he did not want to leave Adam and Eve inside the garden because we can't identify with them until they were ejected from Eden.

In his sermon, Dr. Coffin derided blind faith, which he said was the greatest cause of blind unbelief. But faith was something that Dr. Coffin clearly possessed. Dr. Coffin was brilliant, while I categorized most literalist Christians not only as unintelligent, but also as borderline delusional. So, I wondered what Dr. Coffin would think of my plans to attempt to heal Caroline through a faith healing at-a-distance surgery. Where did that kind of faith fall? On the side of Dr. Coffin or the Christians I usually think of as crazy? Is this what desperation leads you to: a crazy kind of Christianity?

The day before the date of Caroline's scheduled faith healing "surgery," I called her at The Winds to tell her about it. It occurred to me that what I was doing went even beyond the normal (as if there's anything normal about faith-healing) at-a-distance faith healing therapy. The person doing the preparation and liquid therapy surgery would ordinarily be the patient to be healed. But I was asking for an at-a-distance faith healing once removed; I was the one doing the praying, meditating, and attending of "evangelical meetings," but she was the one who needed to be healed. Could that still work? I read Caroline the instructions for the day of treatment and told her to not to eat meat or smoke cigarettes (both things she'd likely still do), light a prayer candle by her bedside (probably against house regulations), wear white, have a glass of water by her bed to drink around midnight, say a prayer, and go to bed early. I hoped that she might be able to follow some of the instructions. I made sure I followed them all.

Before lighting my prayer candle and going to bed at seven thirty, I wrote down this prayer:

January 13, 1987

Dear God,

If you would just touch her with healing tonight, I know she will be healed. Please don't leave Caroline knowing only your judgment, not your mercy. Let her see your love and compassion, which is exemplified in Jesus Christ, your son who lived and died for our sins. Forgive Caroline and me our sins and let her be healed. I know there are others who deserve the relief and mercy I am asking for more than us. But please give it to us, if only because I know you can. I love Caroline. And you, God, are love. I know the love I feel for her is a gift from you. I am thankful for it and always will be. Maybe I have no right to ask more of you, yet I feel I must.

I ask you in humility for more than I deserve or should expect. Caroline does believe in you. She always did. Her belief in you is why she felt she had to punish herself. She felt she was a sinner, so she punished herself because that is what she expected you to do. She forgot about Christ and His message of forgiveness. Healing Caroline tonight could heal her spiritual wounds as well. Please, God. She is only 24 years old. She could have a rich life ahead of her, serving you if only you would save her. I once believed myself capable of saving her, but now I am humbled and realize that only you have that power. And only you have the compassion to save her for the right reasons. My significance comes only from the fact that you love me. Without your love, I am just an insignificant nobody. But I ask you for this miracle because I have faith in miracles. Please heal Caroline and let her live. You can't give up on her now. She's only beginning to understand what has happened to her. Don't make her mistakes irreversible. Save her from death now and I know something good will come from it. It's all in your hands, God. Please let me know what I should do. Guide me through it and do what you will. That's all I can ask.

Amen

I didn't sign the prayer but anticipated that once Caroline was cured I would sign the prayer in blood with a "thank you" to God. It was something I had recently seen Saint Therese of nineteenth century France do in a movie about her short life. I closed both the roller blind and the heavy red fabric curtains and turned off my lights so that the room would be dark, except for the prayer candle that burned on the plywood-covered milk crate that served as my nightstand. At first I didn't think I would be able to go to sleep so early in the evening, but I felt strangely tired and nodded off. As if on cue, I awoke at almost exactly eleven that night and drank down the glass of water I had filled and placed next to the prayer candle before going to sleep. I stayed in bed and prayed some more that God would heal Caroline. I'm not sure when I fell back asleep, but I didn't wake again until seven in the morning.

It was too early to call Caroline since Oklahoma is an hour behind New York. I dressed and went outside for a walk. It was a bright, clear day, just below freezing, in the first light of the morning. Aside from the Korean grocery on 110th Street, which was open twenty-four hours a day, Broadway was empty. I walked up Broadway, past the West End Bar, the University Food Market, Chock Full o' Nuts Café, and the Barnard and Columbia campus gates before turning toward the Hudson River at 120th Street. From there, I could see the gothic tower of Riverside Church. Riverside's Claremont Avenue entrance was open, even at that early hour, and I was happy to find copies of some of Dr. Coffin's sermons available for purchase for fifty cents in display racks to the right of the security desk. I purchased his "Alex's Death" sermon, preached a week after his son died in January of 1983, one from December of 1985 called "God Bless the Cheerful," and the one entitled "AIDS" from January 26, 1986. The security guard did not have a line of sight to the display racks. I left two dollars in the slot in the small brass box between the display racks. It made me smile that Riverside employed the honor system for purchasing sermons.

Columbia was still closed for winter break and there was only one other table occupied by patrons, so it felt fairly private to drink my coffee and read the sermon on AIDS at the Chock Full o' Nuts Café. I used bunches of the rough napkins that I pulled from the chrome dispenser to absorb my tears as I read some of the most moving parts of the sermon on AIDS that Dr. Coffin had delivered a month before I met Caroline.[3]

---

[3]   William Sloane Coffin, "AIDS, January 26, 1986" in *Collected Sermons of William Sloane Coffin, The Riverside Years*, vol. 2 (Louisville: Westminster John Knox Press, 2008).

If doctors don't know the cause of AIDS, ministers don't either. To jump from agnosticism to God's sure judgment, overlooking all the uncertainties in between is (to say the least) dangerous. Beware of ministers who offer you the comfort of opinion without the discomfort of thought! To picture a God of love rooting for a virus that kills people, to picture a God of justice waging germ warfare on sinners and not going after war makers, polluters, slum landlords, drug dealers—all of whose sins affect others so much more profoundly—that's not distortion of the Gospel, that's desertion!

If gay and lesbian couples demonstrate the same deep and abiding love for one another as do straight couples—and demonstrably they can, the evidence is all about us in this city—then why shouldn't the State offer the same civil marriage available to straight couples, offer in exchange for a public commitment, a public contract with all the benefits that marriage entails, including (all-important these days) death benefits? Why shouldn't the Christian church do the same? Is John Fortunato, an Episcopal psychotherapist, wrong to formulate the issue in this fashion: "As evidence increasingly emerges that homosexuality is a natural biological variation in the human species, is it not time for the smug heterosexual majority to give up its self-image of monochromatic normality and acknowledge God's right to a pluralistic creation?"

More than anything else, AIDS reminds us of our own mortality, knowledge we aggressively seek to avoid. It is our need for control, for an orderly, manageable world, that is so threatened by AIDS. So, we project our deepest fears of vulnerability onto those who are suffering most and who least deserve to be abandoned. It is this abandonment that is so heart-wrenching and wrong. Lord knows in this city, it is all too easy to find IV drug users. But to persuade them to kick the habit, or at the very least not to use bloody, dirty needles, is almost impossible; most have reached such a point of despair in their lives that they couldn't care less. And most of us couldn't care less either.

To you members of this church who have AIDS—you, Jim; you, Scott—I want to say, I have seen the grace of God shining in your dear faces.

The sermon ended with a testimony of faith from Jim Johnson, a member of the congregation with AIDS. My coffee was cold by the time I composed myself enough to leave the café and make the walk back home. By the time I returned to the apartment, I figured Caroline would probably be awake. I was excited to call her and hear if anything had changed for her from the faith healing "surgery" I had performed on her behalf.

"Does anything seem different?" I asked.

"I still can't use my right arm. And my leg still feels frozen."

"What about how you feel? Do you feel any better?"

"Maybe. I don't feel too bad today."

"Were you able to light a candle?"

"No. Ken said it would be a fire hazard. Do you think that matters? I did drink some water sometime around midnight."

"No, I'm sure it doesn't matter. I lit a candle for you. I still think it can work."

"Well, thank you for doing this. I have faith in your faith."

"Call me if you think anything changes."

"Okay. Thank you again. I love you."

You really think it can work?

Anything is possible for God. Miracles can and have happened.

Where is God when so many suffer? If God can cure AIDS, why doesn't he? It seems cruel not to. Maybe not as cruel as rooting for germ warfare, but still cruel.

It has to do with faith, Ah Kung. I don't fully understand it. I don't know why God demands faith for miracles to happen. But somehow it seems that faith is what's necessary. All of the stories in the Bible about Jesus's healing center around faith. And that's what the doctor in Brazil talks about too. I know it still seems cruel or at least unfair sometimes when God doesn't intervene and lets people suffer. I'm trying not to question it because I just want it to work for Caroline. I can't really be bothered with the lack of logic or the fairness of it right now.

Maybe something to consider another time then?

Sure. But right now, I just want to focus on believing.

*   *   *

My friend Diana, who was studying the Wiccan religion and midwifery, invited me to attend a menstruation ritual on Friday, the thirteenth of February. Despite Wicca's pagan history and affiliation with witchcraft, I did not see attending the ritual to be in conflict with my Christian faith. I was curious about all religions and beliefs people held and I thought the ritual would be interesting.

It was held in a room looking out onto Broadway from one of the suites at the College Residence Hotel. Thirteen Barnard women, most of whom I knew, sat on the red and black industrial carpeting around a candle burning in a tin ashtray. I had finished with my period the previous week, so I wasn't sure what the ritual was supposed to do for me. But Caroline had stopped menstruating after her stroke so I thought the ritual might do her some good. We were told to bring something meaningful and emotional to us to the ritual for us to burn in the circle.

I brought the note Caroline had slipped under the door to me during her heroin binge telling me to "GO THE FUCK AWAY," which also had a sketch of a face that looked vaguely Asian. I listened politely to the stories told by the other women about the boyfriends or girlfriends who didn't fully value their womanhood. When it was my turn, I told them about how Caroline had suffered a stroke and was diagnosed with AIDS. I told them how Caroline had been addicted to heroin and cocaine and that the dirty needles she used led to both her stroke and her infection with the AIDS virus. And I told them about how I had hoped to cure her through an at-a-distance faith-healing ritual a month earlier. I was grateful that nobody laughed at me or acted like they thought I was crazy. Diana crossed the circle to hug me and help me set Caroline's heroin-induced note on fire and place it in a metal garbage can to burn away. As silly as the ritual seemed, burning the note felt both cathartic and liberating.

I called Caroline on the following day, Valentine's Day.

"I've got news for you," she said. "News you won't believe."

"What is it?" I held my breath.

"I went to the doctor's yesterday, the one who said I had Cryptosporidium. And he said they tested me again and I don't have it anymore. Or maybe never had it. Whatever. I don't have it now."

"What does that mean?"

"He said I still have the virus that causes AIDS, but I don't have an opportunistic infection. So I'm not going to die."

"But if you don't have *Cryptosporidium*, why were you throwing up and having diarrhea?"

"They don't know. Besides, I haven't been throwing up or having diarrhea for a while."

"Since when?"

"A few weeks I guess. And guess what else?"

"There's more good news?"

"Yeah. I got my period today."

CHAPTER 11

THE PERSON
I'VE BECOME

I graduated from Barnard with only slightly better-than-average grades. I kept my anthropology major, though I had lost interest in the subject. I had originally proposed writing my anthropology thesis on Asian culture in New York's Chinatown but I changed it at the last minute to an analysis of lesbian separatism in New York's gay culture. I wrote the whole thesis in a thirty-six-hour cram session. I received only a B for the paper, but at least I graduated on time. That was more than one of my friends could say. Granted, my friend ultimately received an A for her thesis but she didn't receive her diploma until the semester after the rest of us had graduated. I calculated that the difference between getting a B and an A wasn't worth working any extra time on a single paper.

I put more of my heart into the final essay, called "Letter to Mom and Papa," that I submitted for my class on minority women writers. It was a takeoff from an essay included in an anthology of essays we studied in class entitled *This Bridge Called My Back: Radical Women of Color*. The essay in question was called "Letter to Ma" by Asian writer Merle Woo. In my essay I wrote:

April 30, 1987

Dear Mom and Papa,

I'll be graduating next week, and it will be time for me to be
on my own. Your obligation towards me, financially at least, will
be over. I've been supported by the two of you for twenty-one years
now, and yet I feel that you both know and understand so little
about me. Lately I know that looking at the person I've become,
you have been wondering if you made a mistake, bringing me
up the way you did. You've made it very clear that you cannot
approve of the choices I've made for myself over the past four
years, but I know you both still love me. It is because of that love
you've always shown me that I want to try and reassure you that
the choices I've made are not mistakes. I don't doubt that my life
may be a little harder because of my choice to accept who I am but
I wouldn't be able to live with myself if I were to deny the things
about me that make me different and special. I'm sure you haven't
forgotten how I used to be in high school. I hated being different.
I did everything in my power to prove that I could be just like
everyone else in my class. My wish to fit in was so strong that I
hated Grandma and Grandpa simply for not letting me forget that
I was Chinese. Their presence in our house was a constant reminder
that I was different. And I hated them for reminding me. But I've
changed. Now I can embrace my heritage with pride and know
that it's okay to be different. You've noticed the change, I'm sure.
You've even commented on how nice it is now that I can accept
my Chinese background without the shame I once showed for it.
It is this acceptance of myself without shame that has helped me
understand my feelings as a lesbian. Please try to understand that
there is a link. Is there much difference between gay pride and

ethnic pride? My sexual orientation is as much a part of me as my ethnic background. Don't you see that it is a positive thing for me to be able to accept it? If I were to ignore my lesbianism, it would be just as bad as trying to deny my heritage. Accepting it is all I can do to keep from hating myself. When I began to realize that I was a lesbian, I dealt with it much like I dealt with being Chinese. I hoped that I could hide it from everyone else, but I knew the truth when I was alone. I dated like everyone else, not wanting to be different. Sometimes I even pretended that I was in love with a boy, just so no one would be able to guess what I was really feeling inside. I avoided getting close to any of my female friends, afraid that someday my sexual orientation would be revealed. That's why I never could be affectionate with any of my girl friends. I pretended that I didn't like to touch or be touched by them. But it was all a lie. Deep down, I knew that I was gay and thought that maybe I liked female affection too much to be normal. God, I was so obsessed with the idea of being normal. But to be normal you had to be white and heterosexual.

Believe me, I hated the fact that I was gay far more than either of you do now. And I hated myself far more than either of you could possibly ever hate me. You may have known that I internalized a racism against my own people. What I don't think you ever realized, however, is that I also internalized a kind of homophobia that forced me to fear who I was. There wasn't much I liked about myself, except the ability to fake it and fit in. People used to forget that I was Chinese and I wouldn't let anyone know I was gay. I was popular in high school. That really isn't a very easy thing to be for a Chinese lesbian, at least not in a preppy private high school. But I worked very hard at it and I was able to fool everyone.

But then I came to Barnard. Something changed in me. Suddenly I didn't want to be just like everyone else. I felt I could be valued for who I am. I know you, Mom, blame Barnard for my being a lesbian. I've tried to explain to you that it wasn't the school that changed me. But now that I've been thinking about it, maybe there is a little truth behind your accusation. Barnard has definitely contributed to my being able to accept myself as I am. It wasn't until I got here that I started to be proud of the fact that I'm Chinese. Similarly, this place has at least helped me accept the fact that I'm gay, if it hasn't made me proud of it. Self-hate really isn't a healthy thing and, if Barnard has helped free me from the self-hate that characterized my pre-college years, I am thankful for it.

I don't know what made me gay. But I do know that I had less choice in the matter than you may believe. It's me—it's a part of me. And it's nothing for me or you to be ashamed of. In fact, I see it as a means by which I will be able to experience the abundance of life. Being able to love someone is important; the sex of the person you love is not. Since I have realized that I am gay, I have experienced some very positive things—the most important being love. I have been able to admit that I love someone. I never again want to have to lie about or hide that fact. Since I've stopped trying to pretend that I'm going to fall in love with a guy, I have already experienced what it's like to really care about someone—what it's like to love someone. I could never go back to the emptiness of the relationships I used to have with guys. So I've accepted my sexual, no, my affectional orientation. I just wish somehow I could share this part of my life with you, because it is so important to me. I wish you could be happy for me when I love someone and be broken-hearted if that person hurt me. Instead, you have isolated yourselves from this part of my life. I miss your interest.

Maybe things will be a little harder for me in my life because of discrimination—an irrational hatred of me and other gay people which is called heterosexism. It's not so different from racism, or sexism. If I'm going to have to fight against these two -isms anyway, one more -ism is not going to kill me. So please don't worry about me. I'll make it, thanks to a trick you both taught—a trick called survival.

I love you both,

Your daughter, D.J.

My professor gave me an A for the paper as well as for the class. These were her comments on the essay:

D.J.,

"Letter to Mom & Papa" is one of the most remarkable essays I have read, one of the most moving and best written. I'm really at a loss for words—the writing is so honest. I don't mean honest in a mere truth-telling sense; writers often lie that way. I mean honest on the writer's high plane: direct, clear, precise. I mean knowing what one has to say and saying what one means. This is a publishable piece.

—Quandra[4]

While flattered by my professor's comments, I didn't believe her assessment that it was publishable. I wasn't a writer. I wasn't an anthropologist either. I had outgrown my desire to become an archeologist after spending a summer working on an urban archeology project for one of my professors. She had received a grant to have her students sift through and catalog household garbage in a Queens warehouse. It was

---

[4] Printed with permission from Prof. Quandra Prettyman, July 7, 2017.

stinky and tedious work. If that was what archeologists had to do these days, there was no way that was going to be my calling.

As I contemplated graduation, I felt myself drawn to something else—something that had to do with God. I believed that God had answered my deepest prayer in the most miraculous way. Caroline was not going to die, at least not within a few months. I had gotten to write "thank you" to God in blood, just as Saint Therese had done, when I learned Caroline was going to live. This miracle seemed far more worthy of thanks than the one granted to Saint Therese. Her answered prayer had been for a man condemned to the gallows to look at the cross before his execution. Mine was for Caroline not to die from AIDS. God was really showing off for me. The faith healer's instructions had been to "Thank God for the Blessings received, which should always be proportional to its worth." Scrawling "thank you" in blood did not seem proportional enough.

It also seemed that all my admiration was gravitating toward people who served God: Dr. Coffin, Reverend Jesse Jackson, and Bishop Desmond Tutu. What was it about them that moved me so much? They saw suffering and injustice in the world and took action, believing that it is God's will that they do so.

Do you think I could serve God too, Ah Kung?

I think you can do anything you set your heart to.

But is it right for me?

Only you can answer that.

I met with Reverend De Jong, one of Dr. Coffin's associate ministers at Riverside Church and the minister who sponsored me for membership, and asked if she thought studying to become a minister was something I could pursue. I told her how I idolized Dr. Coffin, how I wanted to work for social justice, and how I was feeling a calling to serve God. I told her about my relationship with Caroline and how it deepened my feelings of compassion for people who had suffered as she had suffered—a victim of childhood sexual abuse, drug addiction, and AIDS. I left out the part about the faith healing miracle, still unsure about how Protestant Christians in the United Church of Christ (UCC) viewed such things. She suggested I consider working for the church first before deciding to go to seminary school. I have a feeling she viewed my inquiries as the casual interest of someone who didn't know what she wanted to do after graduating with an aimless liberal arts degree. She told me about a program through the UCC Board for Homeland Ministries, which would place me in a community to do service on behalf of the church—something like a domestic Peace Corp program. That way I could take some time to learn firsthand if a career in the ministry was the right fit for me. I followed her suggestion, applied to the program, and got an eighteen-month placement at a church in Philadelphia. I left New York for Philadelphia a month after graduation. My parents were dumbfounded by my choice to do a volunteer job that paid only a fifty dollar per week stipend on top of room and board. My father took to joking that, at that rate, it was going to take my whole lifetime to make up for the Ivy League tuition they had paid.

My placement put me in a small UCC church in the heart of Center City, Philadelphia. It was near the foot of the Benjamin Franklin Bridge, a few blocks from Independence Hall and the Liberty Bell. I was one of five female volunteers running a summer youth camp for inner city Philadelphia kids. Oddly, out of the five women who were placed there that summer, three of us were gay. Of the remaining two, one was an attractive, tall, and very athletic-looking blond woman from the German-speaking part of Switzerland. The other was a recent graduate from Kalamazoo, Michigan. The two other lesbians were both from the Midwest and had graduated from New England universities. They looked to me like fairly stereotypical lesbians—a little overweight with very short-cropped hair.

The large, linoleum-floored Sunday school room had been converted to our living quarters for the summer. It was furnished with a twin bed and small dresser for each of us. My bed was on the side of the room closest to the volunteer from Switzerland. A bank of dressers separated our beds from the other three. Our showers were in the basement and we had use of the church kitchen when it wasn't needed for congregational activities. Our mouths used to water all night long when giant slabs of beef were roasted for the summertime community festivals down the hall from where we slept. The summer youth camp, Tot Lot, that the five of us ran served about two dozen low-income eight- to twelve-year-olds, free of charge. All the campers were African-American or Latino from the neighborhood north of the church. The kids were all delightful and enjoyed the various activities the five of us thought up over the summer. We took them swimming in the fountains around town and on field trips to museums, movies, churches, and historic sites. We painted a beautiful mural of self-portraits in the lot where we ran the camp. To end the season, we finished off with a concert at which we sang Whitney Houston's "Greatest Love of All" for the parents of our Tot Lot kids. When the summer ended, I felt I would miss our little campers more than I would miss the four other volunteers, whom I never got very close to, despite the close quarters and our shared interest in helping others.

The other volunteers had only signed up for a summer placement, however. So once they left the program, I moved into a small room above the church, across from where a member of the congregation taught cello lessons. From then on, my duties at the church changed. I started serving as assistant to the pastor, a forty-something woman who had been named the first female pastor of the congregation three years earlier.

I also taught Sunday school, managed the winter homeless shelter, and ran a food pantry for homeless and other low-income neighbors. Unlike Riverside Church, whose racially integrated congregation always impressed me—it was in the heart of Harlem, though founded by the Rockefeller family—the church in Philadelphia was uniformly white (except for the cello teacher, who was Korean). Riverside had over two thousands members and around a thousand people attending each Sunday; this church had only about forty members and fewer than twenty might attend any given Sunday service. But I liked my responsibilities related to helping the disadvantaged, particularly the homeless. I wasn't even dissuaded from this work when a homeless, probably mentally ill man slapped me for not providing him more food from the food pantry. In fact, I volunteered once a week outside of my church responsibilities to hand out sandwiches overnight to homeless "street people."

One week, I hosted a class of first-year seminary students from the Lancaster Theological Seminary, located in the heart of Amish country. I arranged for the students to have a chance to attend services at a variety of Philadelphia churches—an African-American church, a Latino Catholic church, a conservative Evangelical church, and a gay church. When I heard some of the students making jokes about the gay church, I kept quiet. I let it go until the next day, when we were having a Bible School discussion about when Moses, who despite the fact that he could hide his Hebrew heritage because he was raised by an Egyptian princess, chose to self-identify as Jewish and pronounced "let my people go."[5] It felt like a sign for me to speak up. I decided to share with the students how that passage spoke to me. I told them that like Moses, I too could hide my true identity from others. But inspired by the lesson, I felt I should embrace my identity as a gay individual and fight for justice for

---

[5]   Exodus 8:1.

my people. Several of the students who had made jokes about the gay church the night before approached me to thank me for helping them see that their prejudice was wrong.

Another really special thing happened during my year in Philadelphia: Dr. Coffin came to make a speech. He had retired from Riverside a few months earlier. Some believed that, in reality, he'd been pushed out by the Men's Group, a group of African-American men whose very conservative Baptist upbringing led them to resent Dr. Coffin's outspokenness around gay rights. He often preached that Riverside needed to be not just nominally "open and affirming," which it had officially become according to a resolution passed in 1985, but to be an activist on gay rights as it had been during the Civil Rights and anti-war movements of the 1960s. Riverside's activism was famous. It was here that the Reverend Dr. Martin Luther King, Jr. made his famous anti-Vietnam war speech a year to the day before his assassination. But the Men's Group saw the struggle for gay rights in a completely different light from civil rights and it caused a rift between them and Dr. Coffin. At age sixty-three, it would be understandable if Dr. Coffin didn't have the energy to fight with this large contingency of the congregation. He retired from Riverside to become the executive director of SANE/FREEZE, a nonprofit advocacy organization that fought to end the Cold War and nuclear proliferation around the world. But it broke my heart when Dr. Coffin announced his retirement from Riverside. My hero and the person I hoped to follow into the ministry was leaving it. So, there was a little consolation when I learned that he was coming to Philadelphia to give a speech at *my* church in his new role at SANE/FREEZE. I personally posted flyers all around Philadelphia announcing his speech and vacuumed the sanctuary so it would be presentable for his visit. I also wrote him a letter telling him how much he influenced my life and how much I loved him (in the nonsexual way a gay woman, forty years his junior, could) and how honored I was that he was visiting my church. When I welcomed him and handed him my letter, he said he remembered me from Riverside from the membership and Bible Study classes I had attended with him. His speech about the insanity of the buildup of nuclear weaponry in the United States and USSR was, of course, brilliant. But it felt like something was missing compared to the powerful messages of his sermons.

The rest of my time in Philadelphia faded like a disappointing dream. It was lonely living in the room above the church. And, although I was told I could have my meals in the parsonage with the pastor and one of the volunteers from the summer program who had stayed on in Philadelphia, I often decided to eat alone, as the loneliness felt more comfortable than making small talk with my colleagues. I took ramen noodles and canned goods from the food pantry and cooked on a small electric burner in the tiny alcove between my bedroom and the room where the church member gave her cello lessons. In exchange for helping the cello instructor out with the Kindermusik (music education for kids) classes she taught to neighborhood toddlers, she gave me free cello lessons some of the few activities that felt like a respite to me. I had to go to all the church council meetings, where they discussed how to attract more members into the church through better advertisements and better signage. To me, the discussions were all missing the mark. I thought it would be better to talk about how we should change our programs to meet the spiritual needs and longings of the human soul for those in our community. I told them about how Riverside met those needs for so many through its intellectually stimulating sermons, beautiful music, community art programs (like the Alvin Ailey Dance rehearsals), and rich social justice activities and programs. But the council was convinced that the problem had to do with marketing. By April, I knew that, if becoming a minister meant having to deal with the politics of working with church councils, I no longer wanted to become a minister.

I'm so disappointed, Ah Kung!

Did you think all ministers would be like Dr. Coffin?

I know he's special. But I guess I hoped the minister here would be a little more inspiring.

Her congregation seems to like her well enough.

That's only because they don't have anyone like Dr. Coffin to compare her with. But you see, even Dr. Coffin gave up on the ministry. I should just follow his lead and get out.

You like working with the children though, yes?

I did enjoy that. But I don't think that's my calling either. It may seem strange, but my favorite part of my job here has been working with the homeless. There's a story in Matthew 25 where Jesus talks about a king who says, "Just as you did to the least of these, you did to me."[6] I feel that the homeless are the "least of these" whom we should care for on God's behalf.

Do you still want to do it through the church?

No. I don't think I liked the politics of it.

When I returned to New York, I got a job working for the mayor's office. It was a little ironic because, while I didn't like the politics of the church, the politics of working for the mayor bothered me less. At least, there, it was *supposed* to be about politics. I was hired on the recommendation of a family friend who was the city council president's chief of staff. I was hired as a community relations specialist for the

---

[6]   Matthew 25:40

Mayor's Office on Homelessness and Single Room Occupancy (SRO) Housing. It was a largely undefined entry-level position that paid a modest salary and made me part of the Communications Workers of America union (though as a political position my dues were waived). Under Mayor Ed Koch, my duties consisted mainly of answering letters written to the mayor by New York City constituents about homelessness. The vast majority of the letters were complaints. We heard from citizen after citizen who wanted us to keep homeless people and programs out of their neighborhoods, which was dubbed the "NIMBY" or "Not in my Back Yard" position. A handful of letters and calls, however, were from advocates for the homeless or other politicians urging the mayor to do more to provide better services to break the cycle of homelessness. I did this work under Koch for two years. Then in 1989, after twelve years as mayor, Ed Koch lost the election to Manhattan borough president David N. Dinkins.

Shortly after election day, Caroline came to visit me in New York. She had come back to New York only once before, two years earlier, when she came for a visit with her mother and an aunt. They had gotten a room at the St. Moritz Hotel in midtown Manhattan. I met them at their hotel room and we all went out for a nice dinner in Times Square. But they only stayed for a few days and Caroline and I had no private time together during their short trip.

This time, she would be coming alone and staying with me at the apartment I was subletting on East Sixty-Second Street and Madison Avenue. It was an old building with only two apartments on each floor. My apartment was on the south side of the building, with hard wood floors and a large living/dining room. The apartment included a baby grand piano left by the rent-controlled tenant from whom I had sublet the apartment with a modest-sized bedroom, bathroom, and kitchen. My parents helped subsidize the 150 percent markup for my illegal sublet.

I shared the apartment with my hound mix, Carson, named after one of my favorite authors, Carson McCullers. I had adopted Carson as a puppy from a no-kill shelter on the North Shore of Long Island. When I picked her up at seven or eight weeks old she looked just like a beagle. But over the first year of her life, she kept growing bigger and bigger until at about a year old she was over seventy pounds and was closer to a small German shepherd than a beagle. I was convinced that Carson's mother was a beagle that had mated with a borzoi. Borzois, also known as Russian wolf hounds, are those giant, extremely powerful hounds that were bred to bring down wolves in the wild for prerevolutionary Russian hunting aristocrats. To me, for some reason, all borzois resembled Audrey Hepburn. Carson too had that Audrey Hepburn look, with a little Marlene Dietrich mixed in around her eyes that looked like they were adorned with mascara.

Carson was the first dog that I had adopted as a puppy and I wasn't really prepared for what it took to train a dog from puppyhood. She was clearly smart. It took very little to housebreak her through crate training—meaning I kept her in her small crate unless I could watch her every move or was ready to carry her outside to "do her business." She was housebroken in less than two weeks. But when she was about nine months old (and already about fifty pounds), she was frightened by the noise of a large truck and she slipped out of her collar and tore down the sidewalk toward oncoming traffic. I was so scared that she was going to get hit by all the cars racing down Madison Avenue that I screamed at her and grabbed her roughly once I caught up to her. It must have really traumatized her. After that, she started peeing on the carpet just in front of the elevator every time I had to take her outside.

After a couple of months of having to clean up her daily messes, I thought that I might have to give her up. But I was already so in love with her that I decided to spend almost a month's rent to hire a personal dog trainer from a highly regarded Canine Academy. The trainer told me that Carson was "crazy in love" with me since I saved her from the scary shelter in which she spent her first few weeks of life. He said Carson must have felt like she "had died and gone to heaven" when I took her home with me. She wanted nothing more out of life than to please me. But he also told me that, because of those first few weeks in the shelter (probably too young to have been separated from her mother), Carson was very sensitive and needed me to be very calm and loving with her. A dog like her, he said, should never be yelled at. All Carson needed was praise and for me to show what I wanted from her and she would go to the ends of the earth to please me. The extensive training package and curriculum I was given from the Canine Academy included a *Far Side* cartoon that showed a dog owner's long diatribe about how his dog Ginger should stay out of the garbarge, while all Ginger could hear was: "blah blah blah GINGER."[7] After four sessions with the trainer, Carson lost her anxiety about going outside and she never peed in the hallway again.

I was so relieved that the training program worked and enabled me to keep her. If it hadn't worked, I knew my mother would lecture me that I had gotten a new dog too soon after we lost our last family dog, Caleb, a male beagle I adopted in my senior year in high school. My mother wanted me to take time to mourn Caleb before getting a new dog. We learned that Caleb had inoperable, advanced liver cancer after boarding him at a veterinary hospital during a family vacation at the Jersey Shore. While he was being boarded, he had no appetite so the hospital did a scan, which showed the cancer had already spread to his liver and other organs. The vet told us that the most humane thing for us to do would be to put him down before he had to suffer any more.

---

[7] Gary Larson, *The Complete Far Side: 1980–1994* (New York: Andrews McMeel Publishing, 2003).

We cut our vacation short by a day and brought Caleb home for one more night. That night we fed him his own whole steak dinner, which was a huge treat for him since we had only ever fed him commercial dog food. The whole family—my mother, father, brother and I—brought him to the vet the next afternoon and we all stayed in the room with him and petted him when the vet injected him with the drugs that put him to sleep. Even my mother cried when Caleb took his last breath, which surprised me. My mother had always acted like Caleb was a nuisance to her. She never let me forget about my signed contract with her (which she even had framed) that promised a half dozen things, most of which ended up being broken promises. But as we watched Caleb slip away, I could tell that in the end my mother loved Caleb too. She also told me how meaningful the experience was for her to watch Caleb be euthanized. It convinced her that euthanasia ought to be legal for humans, saying she thought it ironic how we could be so much more "humane" to our pets than we are to "humans."

One weekend, about a month after we lost Caleb, I tricked my parents into loaning me their car, without telling them I was going to Long Island to adopt a puppy. I didn't tell my parents about my new puppy, Carson, until she had been with me for several months. By then it was too late for them to talk me out of getting another dog.

Carson and I slept together on my crazy-looking round bed that I had gotten from an Indonesian colleague of my father's. His work visa had run out and he had to return to Indonesia and abandoned his furniture. As a puppy, Carson didn't like being left alone for so many hours while I was at work and she chewed holes in the bathroom walls and left gnaw marks on the legs of my landlord's baby grand piano. Carson loved having people around her, so I knew she would enjoy having Caroline come for a visit.

I rented a car for Caroline's visit and got us tickets to see Laurie Anderson in concert at the Brooklyn Academy of Music. After the concert, we stayed up into the early morning hours talking.

"All my friends in Oklahoma are dead. Michael Garrison, a beautiful artist and my closest friend, died in August."

"What about Ken and Blake?"

"Ken died last month. Blake died a long time ago. He had the most beautiful funeral, just like him. He bought twenty cases of champagne just as he said he would, because he wanted us to celebrate his life instead of our having to mourn his death. We had so much fun. But I still cried a lot."

"I'm so sorry. Blake did seem like a beautiful person."

"Keith was the last one to die. He was a fantastic hairdresser. He did my mother's hair too. When I didn't die, I had to move out of The Winds and into an apartment. Keith came to stay with me for a while. He soiled my couch and felt really bad about that. But he died too and now there's nobody left of the people from my support group."

I know what you're thinking, Sya Meh. Are you sure it's a good idea?

I'm thinking maybe she could come live with me now.

It's not like taking care of a puppy.

But raising a puppy wasn't easy, and I stuck with it. When I make a commitment, I see it through.

That's why you should be very sure before you commit.

On the last night of Caroline's visit, I took her to a party at Gracie Mansion for Ed Koch to thank all the staff members of his administration.

After we posed for humorous photos, pretending we were making speeches behind the mayor's podium, I asked Caroline to move in with me.

PART 4:
Partner Me

CHAPTER 12
KNIGHT OF FAITH

The day Caroline arrived from Oklahoma to live with me was St. Patrick's Day. I rented a car to pick her up at Kennedy Airport. Because of Caroline's disability and before such things were outlawed after 9/11, I was able to meet her at the arrival gate. She was the last person off the plane. A skycap brought her out in a wheelchair, marked with the name of the airline, so she didn't have to walk the long halls through the airport. She raised her hand and gave me a big smile when she saw me. I smiled back, wanting to laugh when I saw her in her green jeans and green suede vest.

"Happy St. Paddy's Day!" she shouted. "Why aren't you wearing green?"

"I forgot what day it was."

It was true. The day seemed significant to me for a lot of reasons other than the Irish holiday. An image of the Knight of Faith from Kierkegaard's *Fear and Trembling* popped into my head. Four years earlier, I had given up all hope of ever being with Caroline. Was today really going to be the start of the rest of our lives together? I kissed her on the cheek as the skycap paused to let us greet each other. He wheeled her down to baggage claim and we waited for her two suitcases to arrive. The first was a large black bag to which Caroline's mother had tied a red bandana on the handle to help us distinguish it from all the other large black bags on the conveyer belt. The second bag was an ivory-colored hard case with chrome fasteners. The black suitcase had wheels, so the skycap could wheel it next to Caroline's wheelchair. But the hard case was an old-fashioned bag with no wheels. I had to carry it separately. The skycap was nice enough to wheel Caroline all the way out to the short-term parking structure, so I thanked him with a five-dollar tip.

After we brought Caroline's bags up to the apartment and I returned the rental car, I relaxed with Caroline in the living room.

"Do you really still have that stupid round bed?" she asked me.

"You don't think it's kind of cool?"

"It doesn't work for me. I'm so tall the only way I can keep my feet on the bed is to sleep in the very center."

"Oh, sorry," I told her. "I didn't think of that. We have to move soon anyway. The landlord found out I'm subletting illegally and he's kicking me out. When we find a new apartment, we can get a new bed too."

"That'll work as long as you're okay with me sleeping in the middle of the bed 'til then."

I told her I had made plans for us to meet my brother for dinner at the Empire Szechwan restaurant near his apartment on Columbus Avenue.

"Why do we have to see your brother tonight?"

"I'm excited for him to meet you again after so long. Besides," I said, "I like having dinner with him."

"Why?"

"We're close. He's my best friend and we have dinner together all the time."

"I'm not close to my brother. For obvious reasons."

"Well, my brother's a great guy. And I love spending time with him. You'll see. Not everyone's brother is like yours."

"Okay. I guess we can spend time alone tomorrow."

"It's just one dinner. We have our whole lives to spend together."

My brother and I ordered several different meat, fish, and vegetable dishes, but all Caroline wanted was an order of beef and broccoli. I was impressed that she was able to use chopsticks with her left hand, as she had been right-handed before the stroke. But I couldn't help laughing at her when I saw her place the entire huge piece of beef in her mouth and try to chew it down for the next ten minutes.

"You're not supposed to put the whole thing in your mouth," I told her. "You're supposed to use your teeth to cut the meat up into smaller pieces."

She laughed too, which made it even harder for her to swallow. When she was finally able to get it down, she said, "How was I supposed to know? I'm not 'Chine-eece.' And I don't have perfect teeth like you two. How can I use my crooked teeth to cut the meat?"

I tried to demonstrate the Chinese technique, but she insisted that her teeth weren't straight enough to do it. In the end, she asked the waitress for a knife and fork so she could cut not just the beef but also the broccoli into smaller pieces.

The early years of living with Caroline were a joyful time, but also challenging. Caroline received a government-provided monthly allowance and medical insurance. The mayor's office let me take some time off to help her apply for additional benefits available to her in New York. She no longer used hard-core drugs, like cocaine or heroin, but she was still a pack-a-day cigarette smoker and still craved marijuana. She seemed to need my help in almost every aspect of her care, except scoring marijuana. For that, she was surprisingly self-sufficient. It became one of our most common arguments. But Caroline kept telling me she gave up all those hard drugs and that marijuana helped her cope with nausea from her drugs for HIV (the virus that causes AIDS), so I let her keep that one vice.

We took an apartment in the first place we looked, near the corner of West Seventy-Second Street and Columbus. It was a tiny place with just a small square bedroom, a combined space of about two hundred square feet that served as the kitchen, living room, and dining room connected to a simple three-piece bathroom. It was about half the size of my illegal sublet on East Sixty-Second and almost twice the rent. But with Caroline's new housing allowance and my raise from the city, we could afford it without needing my parents to help subsidize. Living on the West Side again, only three blocks from my brother's place, also felt more like my style.

I kept my promise to Caroline and purchased a regular queen-sized bed from the Sleepy's store down the block. It came with a free steel frame and box spring. We furnished the rest of the apartment with items given to us by my parents and from my friend Josey from the mayor's office. Josey collected donations for homeless programs from hotels that were upgrading their furniture. Her warehouse in Brooklyn was getting full and she needed to make room for new donations, so she let me have a few choice pieces—a tan and brown sofa bed from a run-down West Side hotel and some marble-covered dressers and night stands from the historic Algonquin Hotel. We got a '70s style rust-colored leather sofa, an old dresser, and an orange-and-brown tortoiseshell expandable kitchen table from my parents. Caroline had some art pieces shipped to us—a large framed rocking horse print that got scratched up when the glass frame shattered during transit, a poster of Matisse's *Dance* from the MOMA exhibit, and a signed lithograph (or possibly an original watercolor) by Salvador Dali of two intersecting insect-like figures. I had a framed Masai batik my mother had bought during our picture safari in Africa when I was ten, a poster of a realistic painting of a woman showering, and a long rectangular original Chinese watercolor of birds and a cherry blossom tree, which came from my parents and which fit perfectly in the small overhang near the kitchen. The apartment was also only a block from Central Park, so I could still take Carson there for walks. I just entered from the west now instead of the east. The building had recently been converted from an old Single Room Occupancy (SRO) hotel. I tried not to feel guilty about that fact, since part of my job at the mayor's office was to preserve SRO housing for low-income tenants.

It had been several months since Mayor Dinkins had been inaugurated as the first African-American mayor of the City of New York. Nothing had changed except the mayor. Yet somehow my job changed completely. The top staff resigned while people at my level all kept our jobs. The new team of Dinkins players energized us all. Our new director, Nancy Wackstein, had been on David Dinkins's staff when he was Manhattan borough president. She had authored a scathing report on New York City's failed homelessness policy under Ed Koch. Under Koch, the focus of the homeless policy had been to provide shelter, nothing more. The Dinkins Administration wanted to help people move out of homelessness altogether.

Under Dinkins, the role of a community relations specialist had meaning. I attended meetings of community boards and other consequential government bodies. It was exciting for me to participate in the smoky back room bargaining, where deals were made about which neighborhoods would get homeless shelters, employment programs, drug rehab facilities, and transitional housing programs. I was also awarded a scholarship by the mayor to get a master's degree from New York University's Wagner School of Public Service.

When Caroline moved in, Carson was overjoyed because she no longer had to spend long days alone. Every time I came home, I found

Caroline and Carson snuggled up together in bed—Caroline lying on her side with Carson's head resting in the channel of Caroline's waist. As much as Carson loved me, she seemed even crazier about Caroline for saving her from her lonely days. Now, Carson always sat right by Caroline's feet and constantly licked Caroline's paralyzed hand, as if she were trying to get it to work again. I started working longer hours, often attending late-night community board or board of estimate meetings. There were also classes I had to attend at NYU at night and on Saturdays. Caroline sometimes complained about back pain and menstrual cramps and about a toothache. I was too busy to pay much attention.

One night when I got home late from work, Caroline was lying on the couch with Carson next to her, whining. I took Carson out for a quick walk. When we returned to the apartment, Carson jumped right on top of Caroline and licked her all over the face. Even with all that, Caroline didn't wake up. I shook her, but she still didn't wake up. I pried her eyelids open and nothing seemed to register. She was breathing, but it was almost like she was snoring. I called 911.

Paramedics came and they couldn't wake her either. They got her on a gurney and let me ride in the ambulance with her to St. Luke's–Roosevelt Hospital on West Fifty-Eigth Street. When we got to the emergency room, I had to answer a hundred questions about her health. Thankfully, her mother had mailed all her medical records to me. She gave birth when she was fifteen, then again when she was seventeen. Both live births, both given up for adoption. She dislocated her right shoulder when she was eighteen. She had her stoke at twenty-three and tested positive for HIV at that same age. She was on DDI, an experimental HIV drug that had not yet been approved by the Food and Drug Administration. She took Bactrim to keep from getting pneumonia and amitriptyline for some kind of nerve pain. How much amitriptyline? I thought it was 50 mg. Did I know how much she took tonight? No, I wasn't home.

The wait in the emergency room seemed endless. They had her hooked up to an IV but just left her in a bed in a corridor of the ER for hours. I checked on her every half hour or so. She didn't seem in distress but wasn't waking up either. Finally, at about four in the morning, Caroline started to open her eyes a little when I shook her.

"What's going on?" she asked groggily.

"You tell me. I couldn't wake you up."

"I don't know. My tooth was really hurting and I had really bad period cramps."

"Are you crazy? What did you do?"

"I just took a couple extra amitriptyline pills."

"A couple extra? How many did you take?"

"I think it was three, maybe four. I don't know. I'm really tired now."

"You could have killed yourself."

"I'm sorry. I wasn't trying to. I couldn't handle the pain very well."

By the time a doctor saw her, we drew the conclusion she had simply overdosed on amitriptyline. With time, it would leave her system naturally. She was moved to a semi-private room on a non-acute floor of the hospital. I went home to let Carson out and returned just when the resident and interns were making their rounds. The resident was recommending that Caroline get a lumbar puncture to make sure that nothing else was going on.

I called Caroline's new primary care physician, Dr. Ginsberg, who was affiliated with St. Vincent's Hospital downtown, rather than St. Luke's. When I told him what the resident at St. Luke's wanted to do, he told me to "get her out of there." He suggested I sign her out AMA (against medical advice), because there was no way she needed a painful spinal tap. Dr. Ginsberg took her off the amitriptyline the next day when we saw him for a follow-up. We never could figure out what ailment her previous doctor had prescribed it for. I also got her to see a dentist to fix her tooth and a gynecologist to deal with the cramping.

That was way too scary.

You handled it well. But maybe…

I should pay more attention to Caroline.

Did you expect nothing to change?

Of course I thought things would change.

Then why haven't they?

I have new responsibilities at work.

And your responsibilities to Caroline?

I have them too. I just have to figure out how to do them all.

For Christmas, Caroline went back to Oklahoma to stay with her parents for three weeks. While she was there, we spoke to each other on the phone every day.

"Duke and Duchess had a whole litter of puppies. My mother said we could have one."

"Do you think we can handle another dog?"

"Why not? Carson would love a little sister."

"I don't know. Isn't it hard enough for you to let Carson out during the day? A puppy needs to go out a lot more. And we'd have to housebreak her."

"I can do it! I promise."

I thought of the broken contract I made with my mother to get my second dog. "Are you sure you can handle it?"

"I know just which one I want. You'll love her. She's the cutest liver-and-white female. We can call her Gabby… after Gabriela Sabatini. Isn't she your favorite tennis player?"

"All right. I guess we can get Gabby."

This time, when I picked Caroline up at the airport, she was riding in a wheelchair with a small vented box propped on her lap. She had the biggest smile, laughing uncontrollably as I approached.

"Little Gabby rode on my lap all the way on the airplane. I even opened the crate for a little while and the lady next to me and I played with her. She's the most precious little 'an-hel' you ever did see."

I couldn't believe a dog could fit in the little box on her lap. The box that I brought Carson home in was twice as big.

"Hee, hee, hee. I can't wait for you to see her. You're just going to fall in love."

We fought the urge to open the crate during the taxi ride home but, as soon as we got into the apartment, I unscrewed all the bolts. Carson was loose in the apartment and rushed over to get a look. Carson was nearly twice as big as Gabby's springer spaniel parents. One look and she fled from Carson, yelping like a monkey, "Ay, Ay, Ay, Ay…"

Caroline hobbled over to Gabby and picked her up and cradled her with her good arm. "It's okay, little one. Carson won't hurt you. She's your big sister now."

Carson cocked her head at the strange sound and looked a little hurt by the rejection. Still holding Gabby, Caroline sat down on the couch and told me to sit next to her and then bring Carson up on the couch with me between them. She kept caressing Gabby and speaking to her in a quiet, soothing voice. Carson whined, still wanting to meet Gabby, but she climbed gently onto the couch and sat patiently next to me for almost an hour while Caroline calmed Gabby. Finally, Gabby crawled over my lap to give Carson a sniff. Carson sniffed back, then gingerly licked Gabby's eyes and ears.

"You see," Caroline beamed. "Now we have a perfect little family."

CHAPTER 13

OKAY, I DO

After her near overdose on amitriptyline, Caroline admitted she could use more support and companionship while I was at work. The therapist referred by St. Luke's had been a resounding failure. Therapy only reminded Caroline about painful memories that made her want to escape into a haze of pot smoking. So, Caroline agreed to spend two days a week at an AIDS day treatment program, a few doors away from the Gay Men's Health Crisis (GMHC), who sponsored the program. There she could interact with other people of similar backgrounds in a similar condition. Most had histories of drug addiction and suffered some form of abuse—emotional, physical, or sexual—and would have spent their days in isolation without the program. The program offered many services, including a rich variety of recreational therapy.

On Tuesdays, a retired poetry professor name Lila Zieger ran a poetry treatment program that Caroline attended. Before her stroke, Caroline sometimes scribbled her thoughts on the backs of her drawings, on napkins and in her sketchbooks, often under the influence of alcohol or other drugs. But they weren't really poems. With Lila's guidance and inspiration, Caroline honed her scribbled thoughts into poems[8] that delved into some of the painful subjects she'd tried to avoid in psychotherapy, and with more healing results.

---

[8] Printed with permission from C. R. Hammons, February 15, 2018.

UNTITLED   May 1990

Before, living was effortless…
Reminiscing my kaleidoscope past…
A vacuum for experience…

In escapist effort,
I hid from myself, my truths,
my inner beauty,
my heart and soul.

Now, confronted with death…
I wish to breathe in and out
on a regular basis,
at the top of my lungs.

So this is life…
I need to purify
my existence
in this one world…

—C.R. Hammons

THE WHITE LINE   July 1990

I am where I am today
because of that little white line...
I just couldn't stop doing
that little white line... until
I overdosed that one big time...
Today, I saw a nice, fat line
and I wanted to do that one line.
I said to myself I am stronger
and wiser from the experience,
but I still wanted that one line.
I spent a good ten years
looking for it, and I found
a pipe dream, basing and chasing
the big buzz... The last year,
I spent shooting speedballs.
Then I found that I had
no one to love me... But I
loved drugs before anyone.
Loved drugs and used people...
I'm a changed person today.
Want my relationship to work.
Didn't stray from love,
and I left that one line behind.

—C.R. Hammons

AS IS   Nov 1990

The fabric of my being has gone
through considerable alterations…
and altercations… Changes from ying
to yang… A metamorphosis has transpired…
To the point of walking in comfortable shoes…
I'm past the party scene, the bar scene, the drug scene…
I'm past the escapist effort and I accept myself…
Contented with what I've become from just being,
learning and growing—as is…

—C.R. Hammons

INTROSPECTION   Nov 1990

Learning how to define
God's foremost place in my life…
In my footloose and fancy-free days,
with the ego I had, I felt I was
the center of the universe.
I was only for me alone.
But today I am humbled by
God's gracious gift of life.
Time and space altered my
perceptions about morality and
conscience, and, in time, I grew
a soul…

—C.R. Hammons

AIDS = DEATH SENTENCE   Dec 1990

Too many of my brothers and sisters have
died before their time...
And there is nothing I can do for them,
but to pray to God for strength.
They were not "bad" people.
They were just like you and me...
Yet they were extraordinary people living in
extraordinary times filled with misunderstanding and hate
yet more like FEAR, because they possessed
no knowledge about the disease...
I believe that their deaths put them
in a better place than earth...
loving them is letting go and letting God...
Having AIDS means that you must endure
a slow painful death. And most people
with AIDS shrink down to nothing...
They weaken with each passing day...
It affects each and everyone discriminately,
     uniquely different...
And I am alive today accepting life
on its terms, not on my terms...
At first, I said "why me?" Now I say "why not me?"
It is a very heavy lesson...

A big lesson telling me to take things one day at a time.

Sort of putting life in its true perspective.

We all breathe in and out on a regular basis…

Some of us have more time, others

have less time to do so…

And I will fear no evil…

And dwell in the house of the lord forever…

—C.R. Hammons

In some ways, our lives differed little from those of other young couples in love, living on the Upper West Side of New York City. On weekends, we would stroll through Central Park with our dogs, Carson and Gabby, in the vicinity of Strawberry Fields and Sheep's Meadow, where John F. Kennedy Jr. and his latest love interest might be spotted by paparazzi. We loved watching the talented roller skaters, with boom boxes on their shoulders, putting on a show in the makeshift dance floor on a closed section of the park road. When we could afford it, we treated ourselves to a meal of our shared favorite cuisine at the Indian restaurant that had opened a few doors down from our apartment. It was a lot more expensive than the Indian food you could get on the Lower East Side, but a lot more convenient and quite a bit more fancy. Sometimes, we'd grab ourselves fifty-cent hotdogs at Gray's Papaya at the corner of Seventy-Second and Broadway, or meet my brother for coffee at Café La Fortuna on West Seventy-First Street. Most of the time, I'd cook for us at home—one of my mom's recipes like scallion and ginger soy sauce chicken, or chicken quesadillas, or eggs and sausages. We'd take trips up to the Cloisters, see exhibits at the MOMA, and go to the occasional movie. There was a lot for us to enjoy in a city like New York, even for a young couple without much money.

As a couple impacted by AIDS, we also felt a duty to get involved with some of the political action groups of the time, like ACT UP (the AIDS Coalition to Unleash Power). One of our fondest memories from those days was of participating in an action with ACT UP to "storm" the National Institutes of Health for failing to provide aggressive backing for the development of AIDS drugs and for underrepresenting women and people of color in clinical trials. I still remember the sign Caroline held up at the rally: "Mice have a better chance of getting experimental AIDS drugs than women." I can still hear the words we chanted so relentlessly: "Ten years, one drug, big deal!" The political activism made us feel that we were doing something meaningful and brought us closer together. In the Bethesda Holiday Inn, the night before the rally, Caroline and I played the "quiet game," making love as silently as possible while an African-American couple, whom we'd met only at check-in, slept in the bed right next to us.

But everything wasn't always rosy in our little household. When I was growing up, heated arguments were commonplace in my home and someone would inevitably get a little loud. It happened all the time when we debated politics or disagreed about directions to take or how best to do household chores. In Caroline's family, when someone raised their voice, it meant that someone was about to get a beating. Whenever Caroline and I fought, Caroline would accuse me of thinking she was worthless. She'd threaten to go live under a bridge, like the homeless people she'd say I cared about more than her. The more I wanted to talk through our disagreement, the more she withdrew. If it hadn't been so exasperating, I might have thought it funny to see a short Asian woman chasing after a six-foot tall woman with a cane, limping down the sidewalk in a futile effort to outpace her pursuer.

It's infuriating. I don't know why I don't just give up.

Give up, if that's what you want.

That's not what I want. I want her to understand that I love her. That I'm not going to abandon her just because we disagree about something.

Why doesn't she know?

Maybe I haven't told her.

When my parents were married in 1961, they were both twenty-three. People married young in those days. Thirty years later, I didn't know anyone my age who was married. People just lived together—in sin, so to speak. That's not what I wanted for Caroline and me. I wanted her to know that my commitment was real. It wasn't something I would give up on for a trivial disagreement. Some progressive Christian denominations had started offering what they called "holy" or "blessed" union ceremonies for gay and lesbian couples. I kept pressing Caroline for us to have a blessed union ceremony, just like a straight couple's wedding. Caroline put me off at first, saying that my brain wouldn't be fully formed until age twenty-five. I passed that milestone, six months after she moved in with me. But Caroline still needed more time to get used to us as a couple.

US   Feb 1991

Today, in the here and now.
So full of love, and trust.
I have faith in our
    love and devotion.
Committed to one another.
Strong as steel.
Even in moments of disagreement,
We seem to be two halves of one...
We are the yin/yang of our
    combined existence.
In trying moments, we seem to
Understand the balance of
Our overwhelming need
    to be together...
Work on continuity,
Focus on the process of unity.
Living in harmony...
Learning to love every moment.
Kiss me into sweet submission...
    now.

—C.R. Hammons

FOR YOU...   Mar 1991

My heartstrings flutter...

Be human,

Be able to love unconditionally.

Feel deeply,

Long silently,

Wait patiently...

Waiting for your reply to stir me.

Just loving you for who you are.

Not wanting me to be who I am,

But who you want me to be.

Forcing me to be alone in my space,

Making me question my own validity.

Insecure now...

But not running.

Stopped cold.

Looking inside to the essence of my being,

Barely clinging to the very foundation of life itself...

Mortal me.

Do know that I love you,

am willing to work things out.

I suppose that I am a fixed person...

Oftentimes unchangeable, unbearable.

Tyrannical me,

Ugly duckling me…

Frail and ever so human.

Let your sweetness soften my heart.

Let me lie down beside you and hold you
close to me.

We need time to pull us back together…

Into ONE.

—C.R. Hammons

LOVE IS   Apr 1991

Love is a constantly changing
    state of existence.
A moment distilled in space
    and time…
A sigh, a look, a longing gaze.
A kiss into sweet oblivion…
realizing that living is
    worth it all…
the price you must pay emotionally…
    whole-heartedly.
Life plays out the game of learning
    to love yourself foremost.
And love sends my senses reeling with
    a divine feeling of completion.

With a feeling of being at the
center of the universe...
Knowing she has me
in the palm of her hands.
Forever, together.
Leaving me with a smile... So this must be
what love is...

—C.R. Hammons

I know that Caroline loves me now, Ah Kung.

It seems so.

So I don't see why she doesn't want to marry me.

Is your brain fully formed?

It's as fully formed as it's ever going to be. I'm totally committed to her and I want to have a blessed union to seal it.

Why is a ceremony so important?

Because I think God would like us to commit ourselves to each other, just like with a husband and wife. It's just playing house without a commitment ceremony.

I might like to see a ceremony like that.

You will, if I can get her to agree to it.

WANTING TO RUN...   Jun 1991

From a commitment for a lifetime
'Till Death do us part... I'm talking
tying the knot, gettin' hitched...
you know, married... I thought
I wasn't the marrying kind... yet,
I feel true love in my heart for
her... I must appear to be
some big chicken... still hanging on
to this need to be a free spirit...
Yes, I'm living in sin, but who isn't?
In the eyes of God, I feel love, deep
in my heart, for her... Isn't that
enough? I have to promise love,
honor and respect all the days
of my life?
... Okay, I do...

—C.R. Hammons

Reverend Sarah Zaner was a pastor of the Metropolitan Community Church, a Christian denomination for the lesbian, gay, bisexual, and transgender community. Reverend Zaner provided pastoral care at the GMHC Clinic for people with HIV. Our appointment with her was in the rooftop garden of the health clinic's offices. The sun was low and red over the Manhattan skyline, making the setting on the roof of the five-story building in Chelsea unexpectedly pleasant.

"So, what can I do for you?" Reverend Zaner sat across from us in a matching patio chair.

"Can you do a blessed union for us, even if we're members of another denomination?" I asked.

Reverend Zaner's eyes lit up. "Of course I can. I love planning weddings. I have to say, most of the time these days, it's funerals I have to perform." Her eyes glistened in the light of the setting sun. "What denomination are you?"

"I'm a member of Riverside Church. It's United Church of Christ and Baptist affiliated. They're an open and affirming church and do blessed unions for gay couples. But the unions there are really expensive and we can't afford it."

"It shouldn't be a problem. I can definitely perform the ceremony. You'd just have to find a place to hold it. So, tell me a little bit about yourselves as a couple."

We told her how we met and how we first dated in 1986, just before Caroline's stroke and AIDS diagnosis, how our relationship rekindled in late 1989, and how we'd been living together for about a year and half. She wanted to know what kind of things we fought about and we told her money issues, disciplining the dogs, my work and schedule, and Caroline's use of marijuana. She asked us to tell her how we made up: it took a lot, but we tried never to go to bed angry at each other. Who supported us in our relationship? My brother, colleagues from my work, my friends from school and church, Caroline's friend James, and her poetry instructor. She was satisfied with our answers and scheduled to meet with us two more times before the ceremony. All we had to do was pick our witnesses, the location, the music and liturgical readings, and write our own vows.

My childhood friend Emily took a train down from Boston with her boyfriend to be my witness. Caroline asked my sophomore year college roommate Allison to be her witness. I found a small basement chapel connected to a Presbyterian church on West Sixty-Sixth Street that was usually rented out on Sundays by a Korean church. I could rent it for the ceremony for only twenty-five dollars. The chapel could hold about one hundred guests, but there were only about thirty people intimate enough in our lives to attend. My parents weren't included in that number.

My brother Martin was the videographer. I wore the white polyester dress I had worn to my high school junior prom. Caroline bought an inexpensive white cotton dress from an Indian boutique on Broadway, with a turquoise blue tasseled scarf that Allison helped to tie around her waist. Caroline asked her musician friend James to help with the music. James performed professionally under his mother's maiden name so he couldn't be accused of parlaying the famous last name of his father, a New York congressman. As people took their seats in the chapel, James played guitar while a friend of mine from the Riverside choir played a giant harp. During the ceremony, the two sang a duet of "In My Life" by the Beatles. Thinking of all the friends Caroline had lost to AIDS, when they sang of having loved all their friends and lovers of whom "some are dead and some are living"[9] I teared up a little.

Reverend Zaner read our vows line by line for the two of us to repeat.

Caroline recited:

> You are everything to me...
>
> The sun, the moon, and all the stars in the universe.
>
> And I am ready to continue our combined existence.

---

[9]   Lennon-McCartney, *In My Life* (London: EMI Studios, 1965).

To be officiated today in the eyes of God.

I am prepared to compromise in our disagreements.

I want to learn and grow with you; to share
our sorrows and joys in this uncertain
future.

You are everything to me…

Your eyes, your heart, and your soul.

You make me fulfilled and complete.

I sing praises that I have you in my life.

And I will love and honor you always and forever.

Then I recited my vows:

Every day I have with you is like
a special gift from God.

I am ceaselessly startled by your beauty
—both inside and out.

Through every difficulty you've ever faced
you've come out stronger, even more determined
to live and love the way you know God meant us to.

I am inspired by your immeasurable capacity to forgive,
and I feel sustained by the depth of your love.

I love you for who you are
and for who I am when I'm with you.

As we have our union blessed today, I want to promise you:

    That I will always be there for you no matter what may come

    That I'll be patient with you and understand that sometimes you just need to do things in your way, at your speed

    That I'll try to be understanding when you get upset with me when I want to do things my way, and at my speed

    That I'll never let a disagreement diminish our love for each other

    That I'll love and honor you every moment of our lives together

    And that nothing, not even death, will ever separate you from me.

So, Ah Kung. What did you think?

    Amen.

Chapter 14
LIKE A GROWN UP

It was September 21, 1992, just a week after my birthday. At age twenty-seven, I was going to be a homeowner with a co-op apartment of my own in New York City. Well, technically I would be a shareholder rather than owner, since that's what you are when you buy a co-op. But I would no longer be just a lowly renter. At my mom's suggestion, we had spent the last six months viewing apartments all around the island of Manhattan—from as far south as Chelsea to as far north as Ninety-Sixth Street on both the East and West Sides. With my latest raise at the mayor's office and with what Caroline received in rental assistance through Ryan White grants for people living with HIV and AIDS, we could now afford to buy an apartment for what we were paying in rent, after my parents gifted me a down payment. We saw a railway apartment (named for having no hallways with each room leading to the next) in the famous Ansonia building, where the recent hit movie *Single White Female* had been filmed. We saw a one-bedroom apartment in a high-rise building on West Fiftieth Street that had a view of the Empire State Building. Most of the places were well over the $120,000 I had budgeted for a purchase and had monthly maintenance payments far exceeding the $800 or so I figured in for co-op or condo maintenance fees. We also viewed dozens of crappy apartments within my budget.

So, when we toured the two-bedroom, one-bath, recently renovated apartment in a majestic red brick building, with a two-story limestone base called The New Century, Caroline and I were sure we had found our dream home. We fell in love with the curved bay windows in the corner of the large living room that looked out onto the corner of West Seventy-Ninth Street and West End Avenue. It was one block from Riverside Park, close to Zabar's, our favorite grocery for affordable gourmet foods, and a block away from the #1 subway line that I took to work each day. There were newly refinished hardwood floors throughout the apartment and the updated kitchen and bathrooms were tastefully done. If you opened the window to the kitchen and stretched your head out around the wall to the bathroom, you could even catch a glimpse of the Hudson River. All these positives allowed us to overlook the fact that the building had an eight-step staircase into the lobby that Caroline would have to navigate every day (a challenge with her cane and the weakness of her right leg from the stroke), that it was listed at $15,000 above my budget, and that it didn't have a twenty-four-hour doorman or laundry in the building. Caroline insisted she could manage the stairs with the handrails and we had gotten used to taking our clothes out to a laundromat. We were getting weary of the search and this was hands-down the nicest place we had seen after six months of searching. This place seemed as close to a dream home as we were going to find.

I asked my mother if she thought I could handle going up to $127,000 for the place. She did a quick calculation in her head and told me that to pay $7,000 more would roughly mean an additional $350 each month. The real question was could we handle it. She said, that much more each month would mean we would have to give up eating out, going to movies, getting our coffee at coffee shops, going on vacation, and maybe even paying for premium cable channels. Did we like the place enough to be willing to sacrifice those things for a couple of years until I made enough money to offset the extra expense? The other thing we'd have to keep in mind was that the developer, who had recently renovated the building, was only providing a three-year maintenance deferral incentive, which brought down the maintenance to around $850 (still fifty dollars more per month than I had budgeted). After the three years, the maintenance would permanently go up to more than $1,300 per month. Was I sure that I would keep getting a raise every year, so that by the time the deferral expired, my new income would support the maintenance increase? I had gotten pretty good raises every year. And even though, after the first year, my job category stopped being covered by a union (which had the benefit of collective bargaining), I always received strong performance reviews and was confident that I would keep getting a good increase every year. My mom had the sensitivity not to bring up the fact that there would be an election for mayor in the upcoming year that could theoretically put my tenure with the mayor's office at risk. Both of us hoped I was too far down the totem pole in government for a new mayor to care about someone at my level. I survived, after all, when Koch was voted out.

Caroline and I both said we loved the place enough to be willing to sacrifice some comforts and leisure activities over the next couple of years. So we did a little bargaining with the developer's agent and settled on the $127,000 I had made up my mind we could afford. The agent drew up the contracts and we sent them over to my lawyer, Mr. Benjamin, to finalize before I signed.

Caroline and I were celebrating our good luck in our cramped rental apartment with some Chinese takeout and a bottle of champagne (we would start the belt-tightening once we got into the new place), when I got a call from my mother. She told me that Mr. Benjamin was refusing to let me sign the contract. He was convinced that the developer was running an unethical bait-and-switch scheme. By enticing me with a three-year deferral, he was locking me into maintenance costs that would balloon up more than 60 percent on a permanent basis. He suspected that the recent renovations were nothing more than minor cosmetic improvements that didn't justify the purchase price or the exorbitant permanent maintenance fees.

We knew Mr. Benjamin from when my parents owned a summer home in the Poconos. He was the father of two boys. The younger son, Robbie, was a close friend of mine, and the older son, Jonathan, was a friend of my brother's. During our summers in the Poconos, Robbie and I and another girl around our ages were constant companions, riding our bikes and racing each other around the lake in our dueling Sunfish sailboats. Then we'd sneak into the clubhouse to buy cigarettes from the unattended cigarette machine and chain-smoke them in a makeshift private fort we created out of some open space we found in the bushes between the country club golf course and swimming pool. Mr. Benjamin and his wife still socialized with my parents, even though we had sold the Poconos vacation home years before. Daniel Benjamin, Esquire, was a tough New York Jewish lawyer rumored to work for the mob (though we never spoke of this around him or his family). When Mr. Benjamin said he knew a thing or two about shady dealings, my parents believed him.

What right does Mr. Benjamin have to meddle in my business? As my lawyer, all he's supposed to do is make sure all the paperwork is in order. He's not supposed to worry about how much I'm willing to pay for the place!

But he's a family friend too, no? He wants to make sure you are not making a bad deal.

He has no right to get in the way of Caroline and me getting the home of our dreams.

But your parents trust him. They picked him for you because they knew he would protect you.

Maybe he wouldn't make this deal for himself. But what does he know about what Caroline and I want? He has no business keeping us from our perfect place.

Perfect? Really?

Well the best by far. We looked nonstop for months and perfect just wasn't out there.

Some place better may still be out there for you. Maybe you just need a little patience and some faith to find it.

You're just trying to keep me from being mad.

Stranger things have happened for you, haven't they?

Ah Kung was right. I had gotten weary of the apartment hunt and lost my faith in the universe or God ever materializing my dream home. But Mr. Benjamin intervened, perhaps as God's instrument. Then a month after the first deal fell through, it was either good luck or a cosmic force that got me to see the ad for an even better apartment on West Sixty-Ninth Street and West End Avenue. The ad was in a Monday edition of the *Times*, not in the Saturday or Sunday classifieds where most people place and view ads. The apartment was listed "For sale by owner," and he must have been trying to save money by placing it in on Monday when rates for classifieds were cheaper than on weekends. Luckily for me, fewer people read the classifieds section on a Monday. So, I was the first person to view the apartment and was able to negotiate for the place right on the spot. The owner had listed it for sale at $110,000. I made an opening bid of $100,000, he countered at $106,000, and we settled by splitting the difference at $103,000. The whole deal took about three minutes. Mr. Benjamin must have felt vindicated when he got the contract, saving me $24,000 on the purchase price and over $800 in monthly maintenance fees for the life of my apartment.

The closing meeting was unremarkable but busy with paperwork to sign, including a lengthy shareholders' agreement with all the numerous rules and regulations imposed by the co-op board, such as "No running your dishwasher or vacuum before 8 a.m. or after 11 p.m." I left the meeting with the keys, a pile of papers and building manuals, and a stock certificate for 269 shares in my apartment owners' corporation.

I returned to Caroline and the dogs at our old apartment only two hours before the movers were set to arrive to transport our belongings from West Seventy-Second Street to our new home three blocks south and two avenues west. Caroline was lying on the couch, wrapped in a homemade quilt made by her aunt, with Carson curled around her head.

"What's going on? You couldn't do any packing while I was gone? You know the movers are going to be here any minute and we still have so much else to pack."

"I'm sick. I've been hurling all morning."

"Really? You pick today of all days to be sick?"

"I didn't pick anything. I'm just sick. Period."

"Okay, fine. Do what you want. I'll take care of everything. Again."

It was hectic and maddening to be rushing around while Caroline stayed immobile on the couch but I was able to box up almost everything by the time the movers arrived. And we were able to get everything out of the apartment and into the new place before five that afternoon (which the rules of the co-op required for use of the freight elevator). After everything had been moved, I brought Caroline and the dogs over. To save time and make it easier on Caroline, I used the rickety old wheel chair that we had gotten as a donation from the Village Nursing Home to roll Caroline the five blocks to the new apartment. We must have been a comical sight making the trek from Columbus to West End Avenue, with Caroline still wrapped in the quilt and the two dogs hooked to the wheelchair like sled dogs.

I was filled with excitement being in the new place that I now owned. All I wanted to do was take in the beautiful view of the river and the skyline of Union City, New Jersey, on the other side. But all Caroline wanted to do was get in bed and sleep. It annoyed me that she didn't seem to experience any gratitude for our good fortune and what I had accomplished by becoming a homeowner in a place so much nicer than the rental we had shared for the prior three years. I ordered in food from a decent Chinese restaurant a block away on Amsterdam Avenue but ate alone since Caroline refused to leave the bed. I joined her for sleep well after midnight, as it was hard to come down from my excitement.

In the morning, the view of the river and the Union City skyline was even more spectacular. You could see the red from the sunrise reflected off the windows to our west and on the river itself. It had snowed a little over night so there were patches of snow drifting down the river. I nudged Caroline to get up and see the beauty of our new view.

"Leave me alone. I need to rest."

"You rested all day yesterday, remember?"

"I'm still sick." She pulled the covers over her head.

I pulled them off. "Come on. You're really starting to make me mad."

"What do you want from me? I'm sick!"

Her face was flushed and sweaty. I reached over to feel her forehead. "Oh my God. You're burning up."

"See. I am sick."

"No! I mean you're *really* burning up!"

I rushed into the living room and started opening boxes looking for the thermometer. In the rush of packing, I neglected to label the boxes so it took me four guesses before I found the box with our bathroom supplies. The thermometer read 106 degrees.

"That can't be right. 106? How can it be that high?"

"Don't ask me. Please just leave me alone."

"No, if it's that high, I've got to get you to the hospital."

"I'm not going anywhere. I'm too sick to go anywhere."

"Don't be stupid. You've got to go to the hospital."

"You can't make me." She covered her head with the blanket again.

I threw the blanket to the floor. "I don't care what you say. We've got to go to the hospital. 106 is no joke. We're going to the hospital even if I have to carry you there."

She was crying now, and I almost imagined that the tears were evaporating as steam off her face.

"Come on," I said more softly. "I love you and you really need to see a doctor. Just throw some sweats on and we'll get a cab down to St. Vincent's. Please. I don't want you to die the first day we're in our new place."

I took the dogs out while she got dressed. I asked the doorman to hail a cab on the way back in. When I got back up to the apartment, she was slumped into the wheelchair, wearing her sweatpants and a sweatshirt over her undergarments. The cab was waiting for us in front of the building when we got downstairs. The driver got us to St. Vincent's in less than fifteen minutes.

The wait in emergency was excruciatingly long and I did not feel they were prioritizing the seriousness of Caroline's fever nearly enough. By the time she received a bed and was seen by a practitioner, it was a true emergency. Caroline's fever was still at 106 or maybe even higher and they could barely get a blood pressure reading for her. I watched helplessly as a crew of nurses packed her in cooling blankets and stuck her with a central line. It was almost like a dream—a nightmare—when the nurses started yelling and a team of doctors rushed to Caroline's bedside, punctured the side of her chest and stuck a tube in to reinflate her lung. I wanted to scream when, shortly afterward, they intubated her and connected her to a breathing machine.

When someone finally came to tell me what was going on, all they could say was "she's a very, very sick girl." She was in septic shock and they told me her chance of survival, given her HIV status, was very low. There was very little they could do to improve her chances, except hope she would respond to antibiotics and that the cooling blankets and medications would help break her fever. They told me not to expect too much, that recovery rates for septic shock in a healthy person were only about 50 percent.

After the doctors left, a nurse named Roxanne told me that she'd seen to it to be assigned exclusively to Caroline's case and would care for Caroline all night. I watched Roxanne whispering encouraging words to Caroline through the night into the morning, checking on and changing her IVs and replacing the ice blankets when they melted. They let me stay by her bed in the middle of the emergency room the entire time.

At one point, just before dawn, Roxanne came to me smiling and said, "Hey, I decided to try a bag of ibuprofen and I think that might have worked. Her fever seems to be going down and her blood pressure is starting to go up a little."

By midafternoon, a doctor stopped by to speak to me. "You know, I don't know exactly how or why, but she seems to be holding her own. So, we're going to be able to move her up to intensive care where you'll all be more comfortable."

The move that morning from emergency to intensive care was fortunate because, on that very afternoon, St. Vincent's was designated as the mass casualty center for the 1993 World Trade Center bombing that killed six and injured 1,042 people. It would have been difficult to secure a bed anywhere at St. Vincent's had we arrived after the rush of people from the bombing.

Caroline continued to hold her own after the move to intensive care and, almost imperceptibly but steadily, improved every day. After four days, I was finally able to sit down and write out my prayer to God.

> Dear God,   February 28, 1993
>
> I'm having trouble sleeping tonight as my mind races with fear, anxiety and, thankfully, ideas about how to help Caroline. Despite how hard and scary this all is, what has affected me most the past few days is the realization that more people than I might have expected really are decent and caring. It has taught me that your son's message has not completely fallen on deaf ears these past two millennia. The love I have felt from so many has really held me up and I know that, whatever your will may be for Caroline, the compassion that I have seen all around me has been a tremendous gift. I cannot give up my prayers, however, that you will allow this event and crisis to be another warning and not the real thing. Please, God, let it just be a sign from you that we (or really mostly I) have been too arrogant lately... that I have taken too much for granted and not given enough praise or thanks to you for the gifts and grace you have so generously bestowed upon me. Forgive me for my arrogance and selfishness. Give me a second chance to prove that I can be worthy of your grace. I have not taken the time to show thanks for all that you have granted me and have all too often acted like I deserve special

treatment without earning it. I have used Caroline unfairly to make excuses for my own failings. And have not always been honest with myself or Caroline—or worst of all you. Please accept my confession now and forgive me for my shortcomings and failure to live up to your will for me. Let Jesus's forgiveness extend to me today and let his perfect love cast out the fear that imprisons my heart and soul. Let the love Caroline's family and I feel for her and the incredible love and kindness so many have shown since this all started lift Caroline up in your esteem for her—and let her remain with us so that she can continue to reveal your works through our care of her. And please grant your love and praise to those who have shown such kindness to both Caroline and me, especially Roxanne. And though I ask for more than I deserve, let me borrow Caroline for a little bit longer from you. In Jesus's name, I pray.

Amen

Her time in intensive care was short-lived. She became conscious after a few days. They were able to remove her breathing tube and she had no problem breathing on her own. She still had an IV for massive doses of antibiotics and the days of intubation left her with a sore throat. Her chest tube stayed connected for a few more days. I was horrified by the dark color of the liquid that drained from her chest.

"That must be from all the smoking you do," I told her.

"Give it a break," she said. "I'm not smoking in here."

I thought about the Do Not Resuscitate (DNR) papers I had for Caroline at home and wondered if they would have let her die if I had brought them in. She was alive because they went through extraordinary measures, installing a chest tube and connecting her to a breathing machine when she wasn't getting enough oxygen. If I had showed them the DNR, they might not have taken those measures. But the papers also made me her medical proxy. I was lucky the hospital accepted me as her partner and next of kin without ever showing them any papers.

They took her for a CAT scan to make sure there was no new bleeding in her brain. She was very groggy, almost hallucinating.

"I dreamed I died and they put me in a coffin," she told me. "I saw the church procession and there were angels singing and then I was in a dark box."

They had to roll her by the chapel on the way to the CAT scan and she must have seen them putting on the Sunday service. The CAT scan probably felt like being in a coffin.

"But I'm alive, right?"

"Yes you are," I laughed.

"Okay, good."

"I called your parents and they're going to be here today."

"Really?" she asked. "My daddy said he would never set foot in New York City again."

"Well, I wasn't sure you were going to make it when I called them. You were very sick. It took them more than a day to get a flight out. I thought about telling them not to come since you're doing so much better now. But your mom really seemed to want to come."

"Where are they going to stay?" she asked.

"I'm going to let them have our bed and I can sleep on the fold-out couch."

"They're not used to having dogs in the house."

"I've already asked Martin to look after Carson and Gabby. It's better that way anyhow since I'm spending so much time here."

I met Caroline's parents at the apartment that afternoon. Her father seemed much less able-bodied than I had remembered him. He was still an imposing man, standing over six feet tall like Caroline, and he was heavy but powerful looking. He had been in an accident earlier that year, falling off a ladder while installing heating and air conditioning, shattering his wrist and injuring his spine. So, he had a little trouble maneuvering the bags into our cramped apartment that was still crowded with our unpacked boxes. Caroline's mom was like a whirlwind, pushing boxes out of her way and saying she wanted to get to the hospital right away. We took a cab down to the hospital in the middle of an El Niño storm, with the rains and winds whipping around us. Later we heard that a car had been blown clear off the East River Parkway into the water that day, killing the driver.

When we got to the hospital, a resident was in Caroline's room with a bunch of interns making rounds and they asked us to stay outside in the intensive care waiting room. There was an older Latina woman and her two sons who looked in their twenties also in the waiting room. The woman was crying and the sons were trying to comfort her in Spanish. A nurse came out to bring them into the father's room.

"I can't stand this city," Caroline's father blurted. "Having to share this waiting room with those Mexican thugs is too much for me."

I don't know how I'm going to get through this with them here, Ah Kung. They blow into her life like they've always been here. And I'm supposed to keep my mouth shut when they act like total bigots!

They're scared too. It's their daughter who almost died.

It's not like they do much to take care of her now, other than have her visit them for Christmas and her birthday each year. I can't believe she's not more messed up than she is, with them as her parents. How Caroline grew up without a prejudiced bone in her body is almost a miracle to me.

Imagine if I brought them to our church, with a black preacher and half the congregation being African-American. They'd have a fit!

    Caroline needs them too. So you can put up with them for a short time.

I just hope I don't say something to them I'm going to regret.

I had to put up with them for several weeks, living in the home that had only days before become Caroline's and mine to own. They stayed in our bed while I was relegated to the living room and our dogs to my brother's place three blocks away. I'd be awakened in the morning to the sound of Caroline's mother banging nails into the walls to hang up some of our artwork, running the dishwasher, or vacuuming the floors. Caroline used to tell me about how her mother would act manic sometimes, especially when she was anxious, so I never told her mother about the co-op rules about noise before eight in the morning. I just hoped no one would make a complaint about my new tenancy.

After the hospital moved Caroline into an AIDS ward, her parents seemed less comfortable visiting her at the hospital. Her parents would appear visibly distressed when they came into proximity to some of the other AIDS patients, most of them showing clear signs of AIDS wasting syndrome, being half or less of their normal weight. The friends of the patients were mostly gay and flamboyant. Her parents' voices would get quieter and more reserved as other voices would get louder and more animated around the ward. But while almost every other patient on the ward got sicker from one or another opportunistic infection—pneumonia, Kaposi Sarcoma lesions, or some kind of parasite or infection—and were generally rushing towards death, the IV antibiotics were doing their job on Caroline and she was gaining weight and getting stronger by the day. Caroline's primary doctor came for a visit to let us know that they would keep her in the hospital for another week or so to continue to receive the high doses of IV antibiotics, but there was every reason to believe now that Caroline would return to the general good health she had enjoyed before her bout with septic shock. They probably would never know what caused the infection but that was really of no concern. With that positive news, her parents announced that they would return to the comfort and familiarity of their conservative and simple life in Oklahoma City. After all, it was still winter in Oklahoma and Caroline's father had heating clients who depended on his expert service. They found their own way back to the airport without needing me to accompany them.

Ah Kung, I know that the reason I pray is to ask God to make miracles for Caroline and me. But I really can't figure out why God seems so willing to answer my prayers and not others.

Do you need to know why? Isn't it enough to just be thankful for it?

I am incredibly thankful for it. But it also makes me wonder about God. Take for example our apartment. Yes, it's great that we've got a beautiful place now. It's the home we dreamed about and prayed for. But I work for the homeless. Don't they pray too, or do they somehow not deserve God's favor? If God can answer prayers, why doesn't God do it for everyone? Why do some people have to suffer so much more hardship than others?

Do you think God causes the hardship?

Absolutely not. I believe what Dr. Coffin said about his son Alex's death. When something bad befalls God's creatures, like an untimely death, "God's heart is the first one to break." That, I can get my mind around. But what I have trouble understanding is why sometimes God grants some of us incredible grace. I see all these people around Caroline die of overdoses or AIDS, but Caroline hasn't. Somehow God keeps letting her survive. Don't get me wrong. I don't have to understand it to be grateful for it. But it does make it harder for me to feel that I really understand God.

It's okay to keep trying to understand. If you're lucky, you've only lived a third or less of your life. You still have time to figure it out.

Chapter 15

RUNNING OUT OF TIME

My brother Martin was at our place for a visit. We were having breakfast out in the back yard. It had been a little over a year since we had left New York behind and moved to suburban Maryland. I never imagined I would ever live anywhere other than New York City. I had spent my whole childhood in the suburbs of New Jersey dreaming of the day I would move to "the city." But the city had changed and so had my job. David Dinkins had been voted out; Rudolph Giuliani was the new mayor. And even before that, my boss at the Mayor's Office on Homelessness, Marsha Martin, had left to take a job with the Clinton administration in Washington, DC. Mayor Dinkins had taken the opportunity of Marsha's departure to do away with the Mayor's Office on Homelessness and establish a brand new Department of Homeless Services.

This decision was in direct response to recommendations made by Andrew Cuomo, son of former New York Governor Mario Cuomo. Cuomo had headed a commission appointed by Mayor Dinkins in 1991 to recommend new ways of addressing the "homeless crisis" in New York City. Largely due to a 1979 lawsuit, the city was now providing shelter to more than twenty-five thousand self-declared homeless persons on a nightly basis. But there were still thousands more living in transportation facilities (including subway tunnels), in city parks, and on the streets. Most of the unsheltered were substance-dependent or mentally ill; many were both. Since the early 1980s, the city's spending on homelessness had increased from approximately $7 million per year when the crisis started to more than half a billion dollars.

Cuomo's commission called for making dozens of changes that would shift the focus from warehousing people in expensive shelters to providing services that addressed the root causes of homelessness—factors such as the shortage of affordable housing, the lack of effective substance abuse and mental health treatment programs, dramatic increases in the number of people with HIV illness or AIDS, and a resurgence in the incidence of tuberculosis. Moreover, an overreliance on costly but poorly run government programs instead of on more efficient ones run by nonprofit organizations, such as Andrew Cuomo's own Housing Enterprise for the Less Privileged program wasted taxpayer dollars.

Most of the recommendations were common-sense ideas that the Dinkins administration already supported. There was, however, one recommendation that Marsha and her team did not fully support. This was the recommendation that a new city agency be created that pulled personnel from all agencies that dealt with homelessness and consolidated them into a single department. The commissioner of this new agency would report directly to the mayor. Marsha and the rest of the employees of the Mayor's Office on Homelessness didn't believe that creating a new bureaucracy with hundreds of employees (as compared with eight or so employees in our office) would necessarily improve the homeless situation in the city. On a more personal level, Marsha knew she would never be selected to head the new agency. Her only relevant experience prior to working for Dinkins was as a professor at the Hunter College Graduate School of Social Work.

When the new agency was being evaluated, the mayor asked Marsha to recommend a chief of staff for the incoming administrator. She recommended one of my friends, Bugsy, from the Mayor's Office of Construction. I felt betrayed. Bugsy and I had joined the mayor's office around the same time. We both had earned master's degrees in public administration from NYU. We both were selected for scholarships from the mayor's graduate scholarship program. Bugsy had dealt with homelessness only through a few construction projects for homeless shelters. I worked on homelessness every day. I suspected that Marsha wanted me to stay on as her right hand. But when she announced she was leaving city government to go work for the Clinton administration, her betrayal felt like a slap in the face. Bugsy eventually became the first deputy commissioner of the new agency. I got a much less important job as director for the Office of Technical Support, a tiny office of only three employees.

After Marsha left, the mayor closed down the Mayor's Office on Homelessness and I was the one who had to draft the mayor's letter to us, which was also sent out as a press release.

June 28, 1993

To the staff of the Mayor's Office on Homelessness and SRO Housing:

I regret that I am unable to join you and your friends today to commemorate the achievements of the Mayor's Office on Homelessness and SRO Housing, as you prepare to embark on new challenges within the Administration.

Over the past twenty years, the New York City Mayor's Office on Homeless and SRO Housing—first established in 1973 as the Mayor's Office of Single Room Occupancy Housing—has set policies and advocated for homeless persons and single room occupancy tenants. The office has been fortunate to have had several capable Directors including Elaine Berlin, Lawrence Klein, Judith Spector, Stella Schindler, Alberta Fuentes, and my friends and colleagues Nancy Wackstein and Marsha Martin.

The Mayor's Office on Homelessness and SRO Housing has always been known to have had an exceptional and dedicated staff, and this is no more true than today. You, the current staff members, have served faithfully as public servants on behalf of the City's most vulnerable populations. Your efforts have proved invaluable in advancing the goals and policies of this Administration, and I am sure that I am not alone in wanting to express my appreciation for the work that you have done.

As we prepare to embark on a new era with the establishment of the Department of Homeless Services, effective July 1, 1993, I am grateful that each of you will continue to assist in this Administration's commitment to protecting the rights of SRO tenants and better serving homeless citizens in the City of New York.

Sincerely,
David N. Dinkins
MAYOR[10]

Marsha felt that we had done a good job of responding to the Cuomo commission's recommendations. She'd pointed out that most of the recommendations were simply extensions of policies and programs we had already begun. Or, I should say, Marsha had done a great job

---

[10] Office of the Mayor, Mayor David N. Dinkins, press release, June 28, 1993, Municipal Reference Library.

of pushing *me* to work through several weekends to write much of our forty-page response.

By and large, we stayed neutral on the recommendation to establish the new homeless agency. We simply said we would have to study the proposal. But once Marsha announced her resignation, the mayor took the opportunity to conclude that the new agency was the way to go. It was ironic that, when Marsha left to go to work for the Clinton administration, she was to work for her adversary, Andrew Cuomo, who by then had been appointed assistant secretary of Housing and Urban Development. It was also ironic that Andrew Cuomo didn't seem to have enough clout in the Clinton administration to propose a new consolidated federal agency for homelessness at the national level.

At the Federal Interagency Council for the Homeless, Marsha was a one-woman show. She was asked to coordinate the various federal agencies that had a role in combatting homelessness. Marsha didn't have a job for me, but we kept in touch and she sympathized with me when I complained that it felt like Giuliani's only plan for addressing homelessness was to arrest them to keep them from living on the streets. I didn't want to work for that kind of mayor or for an agency that treated the homeless like criminals rather than like people in need of help. When an opening came up as head of programs at a nonprofit advocacy organization supposedly founded through a bipartisan collaboration between the wife of a democratic vice president and wife of a republican secretary of state, Marsha recommended me for the position. She even let me live at her home in Washington, DC, for the month it took me to find a place for Caroline, me, and the dogs. Eventually, we settled in a small brick rental home in suburban Maryland about thirty minutes from my job at Sixteenth and K Street in Washington, DC, where I worked two blocks north of the White House.

That morning, as we had breakfast on our lawn in Silver Spring, Maryland, I told my brother about a strange dream that had awakened me. Todd Carr, a boy to whom I had once written a love letter in the summer between sixth and seventh grade, was goose-stepping under the staircase of my brother's and my childhood home. With each goosestep he was kicking me in the head. I couldn't imagine why I might be dreaming about Todd Carr. After he never responded to the embarrassing letter I wrote that summer at tennis camp, I hardly even talked to him or ever really thought about him.

"Isn't the president of your organization named Todd?" my brother asked.

"Yes, Todd Kelley."

"Maybe your subconscious brain is telling you that Todd Kelley is a fascist and you feel like he's kicking you in the head."

Wow. It sounded right. My job was making me increasingly uncomfortable. I imagined that working for a nonprofit homeless advocacy organization would be more rewarding than doing government work. But the work really meant spending most of my time trying to convince other small, resource-strapped nonprofit homelessness organizations around the country to become members of our organization. They would sign up for memberships to receive our newsletter and would pay to attend conferences and workshops that I arranged around the country. Some of the conferences and workshops I organized felt like they brought some value. I held workshops in Houston, Atlanta, and New York City. The one in New York ended with a concert by legendary folk singer Pete Seeger. It was an emotional event, since it was the day after the Oklahoma City bombing of a federal building, where 168 people were killed, mostly federal employees, but also fifteen children attending day care in the building. I had also organized our massive annual membership conference, where both Marsha and Assistant Secretary Cuomo gave powerful keynote addresses. Another highlight of the conference was a lively "Fred Friendly-style Socratic Seminar," a moderated roundtable dialogue I had conceived and scripted. It featured a distinguished and diverse panel of homeless advocates and service providers, media personalities, government officials, and journalists discussing the hypothetical of solving homelessness in the United States. The conference was successful and very well received by our members. I, however, was becoming increasingly unhappy at my job.

And yes, my biggest objection had to do with Todd Kelley. As president of the organization, he earned as much as the president of the United States. Yet, he was only in the office a maximum of two to three days a week since his permanent residence was still in Connecticut and he chose to limit his commutes to the middle of the week. I never really knew what he did or how he contributed to our mission. Moreover, I knew we were paying for his weekly commuting costs and temporary residence in Washington, DC. I imagined how the hard-earned membership income I brought in from struggling nonprofits could be better spent than paying for his salary and weekly expenses.

I was working long hours for something I didn't really believe in and neglecting Caroline at home in the new place I had dragged her to. When we arrived in Washington, DC, I brought Caroline to the Whitman Walker Clinic, the largest HIV and AIDS service provider in the greater Washington area, to get her health checked. Her T cells had dropped to ninety-two. T cells are a measure of one's immune system and in a healthy person they number between 500 and 1,700. Any number below one hundred defines a patient as having officially gone from HIV illness to "full-blown" AIDS. We were running out of time and treatment options.

That's when we decided to go with a controversial new primary care physician in Washington, DC. We were ready to seek aggressive treatment for Caroline, and Dr. Gary Banks was reputedly the doctor to see if you wanted to put up a fight. Even other HIV specialists conceded Dr. Banks's uncanny intuition about AIDS.

When we started seeing him, he explained that his practice had taken a hit recently from a multi-million dollar malpractice suit, which he'd lost. He'd been sued by a gay ex-priest, whom Dr. Banks had treated for HIV infection for five years. The ex-priest had subsequently tested negative for HIV infection, and he claimed that Dr. Banks had treated him—with many medicines amounting to poison—for a disease he never had. The whole case seemed fantastic to me. I wondered why someone who had once been a priest, whose lover had died of AIDS and who begged Dr. Banks to treat him aggressively and save his life, would choose to sue him rather than thank him for possibly having cured him. At the trial, Dr. Banks's lawyer argued that the ex-priest had actually been cured of the virus by Dr. Banks's aggressive treatment. They insisted that, when the plaintiff had come to Dr. Banks, he had tested positive for HIV on four prior occasions, a claim supported in testimony by both the plaintiff himself and his previous physician. The jury ultimately rejected the claim that Dr. Banks might have actually cured the ex-priest. They found it too extraordinary. They didn't believe AIDS could be cured, even though medical literature had reported a handful of cases in which an HIV-positive patient suddenly, somehow, became HIV negative. They awarded the ex-priest $4.1 million in damages.

I, however, preferred to believe in the possibility (remote as it may have been) that Dr. Banks could have cured his patient and hoped that his aggressive treatment of Caroline might give her an equally good outcome.

Some of Dr. Banks's treatments taxed Caroline severely. He put her on several experimental, off-label treatments, including thalidomide, the drug given to women experiencing morning sickness in the 1960s, which had resulted in "thalidomide babies," children born with missing or significantly stunted arms. Dr. Banks believed that thalidomide could ease AIDS symptoms. In his view, as long as Caroline was not planning to get pregnant, she could take it without any negative impact. He also put her on human growth hormone as well as interluekin-2, which causes severe and unpleasant flu-like side effects. Both of these treatments had to be taken as injections. The injections had to be self-administered when I traveled for work, which was often.

If Caroline now had "full-blown" AIDS, how could I justify spending most of my time at a job I didn't really believe in? I felt that my whole purpose in life was to help other people, but I wasn't even around to help the most important person in my life. The dream about "Todd" goose-stepping and kicking me in the head made me really uneasy.

Why not quit, if it doesn't feel right anymore?

What would I do if I quit? I dragged Caroline down to Washington for this new job. What would she think—what would my parents think, for that matter—if I just up and quit without having another job?

But isn't Caroline more important to you than your job?

I have responsibilities though. I still have to pay the rent, feed us, and keep us in clothing.

Buddha said that suffering comes from clinging to possessions. What does your Bible say about it?

Well, you got me there. Jesus said, "Is not life more than food, and the body more than clothing? Look at the birds of the air; they neither sow nor reap nor gather into barns, and yet your heavenly Father feeds them.

Are you not of more value than they? And can any of you by worrying add a single hour to your span of life?"[11] But that's all very well and good for Jesus to say and for people to believe in theory. But I have to be practical too. I can't just ignore those things.

You can if you truly have faith.

My brother went back to New York without my telling him what I was considering. I felt very scared, but the Monday after he left, I submitted my resignation to the nonprofit after only a little more than a year working there. I wrote a letter to their board of directors telling them that I did not feel that paying for Todd Kelley's high salary and his expenses to commute from Connecticut were a good use of the nonprofit organization's funds and I hoped that they would consider changes to the organization after my departure.

Meanwhile, two days after my parents and brother left for a summer vacation in Italy, I learned that my grandfather, George, my mother's father, had died. I had let my family leave the country without telling them of my resignation. I didn't want to worry them; I also didn't want them to try to change my mind. My grandfather had been in a nursing home in New Jersey from complications from diabetes, including congestive heart failure, and my mother had a chance to say goodbye to him just before leaving on her trip. He had told my mother that he dreamed about her late mother, his wife Celia, and that Celia had told him it was time for him to join her now. My grandfather said he was ready. He also told my mother that she should not cancel her trip, since they had made their reservations so much earlier and it would be a shame for her to lose what they had pre-paid for the trip just to attend his funeral. It was enough for them to say their goodbyes before she left

---

[11] Matthew 6:25–27.

for Italy. But it made me sad that my mother was not at his side when he died, even if her siblings were there.

I couldn't help thinking about a story my mother had told me about my great-great grandfather. When his first wife died, he remarried a woman who treated her new stepchildren like strangers and interlopers. His oldest son decided to protest his father's decision to remarry this awful woman by way of a hunger strike, and he subsequently died. After his brother's death, my great-grandfather swore to his father that he would never see him again, even on his deathbed. In Chinese culture, for a child to refuse to see a parent on their deathbed is considered a terrible dishonor—a signal to the whole community what a terrible person that parent must be. But my great-grandfather later regretted his decision because his own fate was to die without his children beside him. When he died, the political situation in post-revolution communist China prevented his children from returning to Shanghai from Hong Kong, where they had all fled to avoid the Cultural Revolution. So, as my great-grandfather had seen to it that his father would die without his only living child by his side, his punishment for committing that dishonor was to die without his own children. Knowing that my mother was in Italy when my grandfather died made me wonder if the family "curse" had somehow continued into the next generation.

Caroline and I made the four-hour drive back to New Jersey so I could be the only member of my mother's nuclear family to attend the funeral. It was a Christian funeral, presided over by the minister of the Presbyterian church that had helped provide pastoral care visits and transportation to my grandmother Celia when she was dying from Alzheimer's. The pastor gave the eulogy and recounted how my grandfather George had told him that he didn't believe in organized religion. Nevertheless, the pastor felt that George was a deeply spiritual person and often engaged in lengthy philosophical and theological discussions with the pastor. He said that

George expressed great appreciation for the Christian kindness shown to Celia by his church and that they were honored that George had made generous donations to the church to support their mission.

The funeral took place a week before my thirtieth birthday. While my grandfather died in his mid-eighties, death always made me question whether I was living my purpose in life. Maybe I would get to live into my eighties, but surely Caroline wasn't going to now that she had crossed the line into an official AIDS diagnosis. Saying goodbye to my grandfather made me feel it was the right decision to take a pause and figure out what was important to me. I had had a decent career in government and the nonprofit sector. Now, I had just quit my job without having a clue about what I was going to do next. Caroline was on Medicare and Medicaid. She also received benefits from Social Security, as well as a Section 8 housing voucher that helped her cover her half of the rent. She didn't need my income or insurance to receive medical care and money for housing and modest living expenses. I knew I could cash in my 401K plan from my years of working for the city. But how long would that keep me afloat? What else could I do with myself to earn a living and still be able to take care of Caroline and her health needs?

By that time, Marsha was no longer working for Andrew Cuomo. She had made the mistake of telling him, one day during a heated argument, that nobody cared who his father was. It seemed she was wrong. Not only did people in Washington care about who his father was, but they cared who he was married to—one of Bobby Kennedy's daughters and sister to Maryland Lieutenant Governor Kathleen Kennedy Townsend. Cuomo never fired Marsha, but she found herself listened to less and less often. When a job opened up in the Department of Veterans Affairs, she quietly moved on to a new position.

*   *   *

September 14, 1995: Today I am thirty years old. And I find myself for the first time in my life unemployed and without real direction. I'm reading a book that says, "Creativity is God's gift to us. Using our creativity is our gift back to God."

Is this what they call mid-life crisis, Ah Kung?

If you only live to sixty, perhaps. But if you live as long as I did, you have many more years before you reach mid-life.

I don't mean literally, Ah Kung. I mean, am I being crazy throwing everything away to try to discover what my gift is?

Crazy maybe. Brave maybe. When Caroline wasn't in your life, it was good of you to dedicate your life to helping strangers. But with Caroline's life in danger, it would be wrong to care more about the lives of distant people than the person you've committed your life to.

Maybe I should just ask Marsha to give me a job with Veterans Affairs. At least I'd be making money and still doing some good.

Do you feel that your gift is as a government bureaucrat?

Why not? I did it pretty well for six years. And I liked working for Marsha. She taught me a lot and challenged me to make stronger arguments. I couldn't have written the response to the Cuomo commission recommendations without all her challenges. Even though I didn't get any credit for our report, I was pretty proud of my work on it.

It's easier to stay in the background behind someone else. But finding your own voice and speaking for yourself takes real strength and courage. You've already made the first step by leaving your job. Why not see it through?

Because what if it's just a big mistake? What if I am just meant to be a bureaucrat?

That would be a surprise.

The question of the gift occupied a lot of my thoughts. It made me think about Jesus's Parable of the Talents from Matthew 25: 14–30 in the New Testament. Even though in the parable, "talents" are coins made of gold or silver, it always struck me that the parable could actually have been talking about actual talents, as in gifts. In the parable, a master gives three of his slaves talents each according to their abilities. To one slave, he gave five talents; to another he gave two talents; and to the third he gave only one. The one who received five talents immediately went off to the market and traded with them and earned five more. The one who received two did similarly and made two more. But the third one was afraid of losing what his master had given him. So he dug a hole in the ground and buried it. I didn't think the parable was about how the rich deserve to get richer, since Jesus also said, "It is easier for a camel to go through the eye of a needle than for someone who is rich to enter the kingdom of God."[12] The parable seemed to be Jesus calling on us to invest our gifts on behalf of God. Not only was it telling us that we ought to invest in proportion to what God gives us but also that the more we contribute, the more we will be given to contribute with.

I felt that God had blessed me in so many ways and had given me so many gifts already. If I invested my talents, as in the parable, what would that look like?

I started by investing time in my relationship with Caroline. I signed us up for a support group with the Whitman-Walker Clinic for couples where one was HIV positive and one was HIV negative. Somewhat humorously, they called it the group for "discordant" couples. There were two other couples in the group, both gay male. Caroline and I had been together the longest and we were the only ones who had entered into our committed relationship with advance knowledge of our "discordant"

---

[12] Matthew 19:24.

status. The other two couples had the added complication of infidelity that resulted in one of the partners becoming infected. I had always heard so much about the superficiality of gay male relationships. But these two relationships didn't seem superficial at all. Both these couples were sticking together despite almost overwhelming obstacles. I was impressed with the commitment of the other two negative partners who had enough love to forgive and care for their partners even after the betrayal and risk to their own health. Sex between men is one of the most common ways of transmitting HIV, while sex between women is actually one of the least common. I never really feared getting HIV from Caroline, even though it was always slightly nerve-racking when I would get tested every two or three years. I was surprised that these negative partners didn't express any real anger or blame at the other half of their couple. What I saw much more of was the love for and fear of loss of their partners. It was comforting to hear someone else being worried or even getting angry about their other half's weight loss or forgetting or otherwise neglecting to take their twice-daily regimen of eight to twelve pills. I related to the laments that a skipped meal or missed dose felt like a lack of love. It didn't seem crazy to me when someone would say, "If you really loved me, you'd try harder to stay alive."

But as much as I appreciated the support and reassurance I got from getting to know these other couples, I was conscious about getting too close. It was distressing to hear about how the other two HIV-positive partners were not responding well to their treatment. I felt guilty that Caroline's health seemed to be holding steady with all the treatments Dr. Banks was throwing at her, while the more conventional treatments the other two received no longer seemed to be working. One of them got a brain infection, the other skin lesions. Caroline reminded me about how hard it was for her to lose every one of her fellow support group and AIDS hospice residence members to death in Oklahoma—about one hundred of them over the four years she was there. She didn't want to start down that road again. So when the support group ran its course after eight weeks, we didn't keep in touch with the other couples.

I also wanted to explore my spirituality and find a new church. It was difficult for me to compare any place to Riverside Church in New York. The Reverend Dr. James Forbes had replaced Dr. Coffin at Riverside. Dr. Forbes was the first African-American to be selected as senior minister of such a large, historic, and interracial church. And while it took me a little while to warm up to Dr. Forbes, by the time we left in June of 1994, I came to love his preaching. Riverside was where I really became a Christian. It was my church. I had even taken a short stint as the chair of Riverside's Maranatha Committee (its LGBT group) where I'd made some close friends, and I rarely missed a Sunday service. I had a hard time picturing myself anyplace else. No church in the Washington, DC, area in my mind could compete with Riverside.

I did have a mesmerizing experience attending an outdoor service in the woods of rural Virginia with the administrative assistant from the homeless nonprofit. Tina was a young African-American single mother who was raising a baby to whom she'd given birth while I was at the nonprofit. She knew I was interested in finding a new church home and she told me that the Save the Seed Ministry had turned her life around. The service reminded me of the Southern revivals I had heard about. There must have been about two thousand people in those woods that Sunday and people regularly shouted out or "spoke in tongues" throughout the service. Dozens of attendees were paraded up to the charismatic minister, accompanied by their families—drug dealers, drug addicts, gang members, and other criminals—all to be saved by accepting Jesus Christ into their lives. The families and the sinner were all in tears as the preacher asked if the sinner was ready to give up his or her life of sin to be saved. There was shouting—Halleluiahs and Amens—all around the grounds. Each time, the preacher would strike the sinner on the forehead and he would collapse into the arms of his family before being dragged away to a tent off in the background. It was moving to witness but also a bit scary. Where were the sinners being taken and for how long? Tina told me she had been addicted to drugs and been promiscuous until she came to Save the Seed. I wanted to ask her more about what happened after the "saving" ceremony but thought it might be too personal or too proprietary to their methods. A few of the sinners were homosexuals or "sodomites" as the preacher and families called them. While I was moved by the way it seemed some of these truly lost people might be able to turn their lives around through this ministry, I knew it would not do for me.

Why do you think it helped your friend?

I think it gave her a place where she felt loved. I also think there's something about believing you are forgiven that can free you to make changes. It was powerful to witness. Take the gang member who murdered a rival gang member. If that young man can truly be saved, it would be amazing.

You don't think he deserves to be punished?

I want him never to kill again. If I thought sending him to prison would do that, then sure. But chances are, if he went to prison it would not change his life. He'd probably still be connected with a gang and still be fighting with rival gangs inside prison. Most young people who go to prison come out even more hardened. But if this ministry can tear him away from his gang and turn him into someone who does not want to kill or commit other crimes again, I think it's a far better outcome than prison.

You think he should be forgiven?

It may be the only thing that can allow him to change. If he can believe he's forgiven for what he's done in the past, he can imagine a different future for himself. It takes love to break the cycle of violence, not punishment and more violence. I can see this ministry bringing a lot of good to the community. But they're just wrong about their view on gays and lesbians.

How do you know?

Because I believe my love for Caroline comes from God. It doesn't go against God. I'm pretty sure that God made all of humankind—people of all races, religions, and sexual orientations. God made me gay just like God made others straight. And as Dr. Forbes says, "Our sexual orientation is a gift of God's creativity."[13]

You believe it's not a choice?

I do now. I tried hard to be straight but that wasn't what was natural for me. Even zoologist Desmond Morris wrote in "The Naked Ape"[14] that homosexuality is a natural variant in many species. At the same time, he pointed out that a homosexual is no more reproductively aberrant than a celibate monk or priest. And you wouldn't consider a monk or priest to be sinning against God for not procreating. No, the only behavior in my mind that goes against God is when we do harm to one another.

Didn't you hurt your mother when you shared your news?

It wasn't me hurting her. Maybe she was sad that her dream for me was broken. She had to mourn the loss of grandchildren I would never give her, at least in any conventional way she imagined. And I think it hurt her that other people might not treat me the same as straight people. But

---

[13]   James Forbes, *Whose Gospel?: A Concise Guide to Progressive Protestantism* (New York: The New Press, 2010).

[14]   Desmond Morris, *The Naked Ape: A Zoologist's Study of the Human Animal* (London: Cape, 1967).

that's not my fault. That's on the people who don't want to treat me as an equal.

So your quest for a new spiritual home continues?

Yes, I think it has to.

PART 5
.... Me

CHAPTER 16

A HAMSTER'S WHEEL

The moment Ken announced his resignation, I knew in my gut that I would become the new manager of document control. I had been employed as a senior document control specialist for a little less than a year. I was working at a small biotechnology contract lab and manufacturing company in Rockville, Maryland. Officially, Ken was the manager of the group, but I felt like I was the one who did all the work. I was the one who came up with all the new templates and processes and the person everyone who wanted anything documentation-related came to for help.

I was not a big fan of Ken's. Only a month earlier, I had gotten a lot of satisfaction out of shutting him up when he reprimanded me for coming in to work an hour late. Ken started delivering a lecture to me as to why it was important to be on time and, especially that morning, since the company had just announced the consolidation of its contract manufacturing company under the same corporate umbrella. I told him that my close friend Stephen had died the night before, and I didn't get much sleep.

Stephen Smith was the only person with AIDS who Caroline and I allowed ourselves to get close to in Washington. He was an activist with ACT UP and ran the DC Cannabis Buyers' Club out of his small apartment near DuPont Circle. Stephen was the one who recommended Dr. Banks to Caroline. At first, he took the same types of experimental treatments as Caroline. But Stephen had chosen to discontinue the often-debilitating treatments about a year earlier. He refused to take any more toxins concocted by pharmaceutical drug companies. But he did accept from me a tin-covered plastic cup of Ganges River water my mother had brought back from her vacation to India. He drank it down enthusiastically, nearly choking on the water. I thought it was disgusting to drink water from a river where people burned their dead, despite the label's claim that it was "purified." But Stephen thought the water was holy and brought him more gently toward the state to which he would soon be going.

We watched him get weaker and thinner with each passing week. Sometimes, when we visited him, it seemed that he was losing his mind. He said he regularly received visits from the many friends who had passed before. He told us his cat gave him a deep tissue massage every night. We hated to see him give up. Dr. Banks had Caroline on a new regimen of experimental treatments. They were based on the research of Dr. David Ho, who had begun publishing papers on a new strategy to attack HIV infection with a multiple "cocktail" therapy treatment regimen, similar to a known method for treating cancer. At the same time, a new class of HIV drug called protease inhibitors (PIs) was being developed. PIs worked by blocking the enzyme HIV needs to replicate itself. The first of these PIs was just then undergoing clinical trials, and Dr. Banks had gotten Caroline on it through a compassionate use program from the drug's manufacturer. Stephen considered all those drugs to be poison, however, and he wasn't going to put them in his body anymore. He couldn't get much food into his body either, even though all his friends brought him food every day. His fridge and garbage cans got fuller and fuller as Stephen got thinner and thinner.

The night Stephen died, Caroline and I went to see him at Georgetown Medical Center. We had just come from seeing Boy George perform at a small club in the city near the hospital. There were two other friends there, but Stephen was too weak to speak to any of us. He looked like the emaciated survivors of Nazi concentration camps. His face had the same look of relief and gratitude and we knew that he would be released soon too. When we said our goodbyes to him, Stephen could say nothing back. He closed his eyes and I was glad he couldn't see the tears in our eyes. About an hour after we returned home, the phone rang with the news that Stephen was gone. Caroline and I went out to our back porch. As we stood there, a shooting star crossed the entire night sky. It felt like Stephen saying his goodbye.

I didn't tell all this to Ken when he reprimanded me for being late, but I did tell him my friend had died, and it shut him up. So, I wasn't at all sorry to hear the news that Ken was leaving. He was a well-spoken, fancy-dressing African-American who knew how to toot his own horn and never deigned to do the work of the people he managed. He moved around from job to job every two to three years, leaving just before anyone caught on that he didn't really do anything. He was going to be leaving us to head up a new dossier submission publishing unit for a big pharmaceutical company—a job with more prestige, pay, and employees. This was typical for Ken's career. He had the remarkable ability to parlay his latest unremarkable tenure into an opportunity for advancement at a bigger, better company. But I knew his move was going to end up being good for me. It would allow me to get myself out of the mess I had gotten myself into from the almost two and a half years I had spent without an income, trying to "find my calling." Those days of wandering in the wilderness were coming to a close. I felt that, finally, I had landed someplace where I could build a career in a growing industry.

So, this is really what you want?

It's what'll be good for me, Ah Kung. I'm going to finally be able to get myself out of all that debt I ran up. I'm going to be able to take care of Caroline and have some financial security.

What about the other things you hoped to explore?

I tried. I gave myself more than enough time for God's will to reveal itself to me. But all I got from it was a mountain of debt and a bunch of failed ventures.

Really? That's all you got from it?

That's how it felt.

Funny. I assumed you got more out of it.

What started out as a break I thought I would be taking for a few months dragged on for a little over two years. In this time, I read or reread everything I thought could shed light on what I felt God might be calling me to do: from classic writings by Plato, Lao Tsu, St. Augustine, de Tocqueville, Thoreau, Kierkegaard, Tolstoy, and Dostoevsky to more modern writings by Aldous Huxley, Carlos Castaneda, Dr. Coffin, and James Redfield. I attended lectures (in addition to reading the books) by Rabbi Harold Kushner, who wrote *When Bad Things Happen to Good People*, and Marianne Williamson, author of *Return to Love: Reflections on the Principles of a Course in Miracles*. I tried to inspire myself through several of the memoirs by family friend Gordon Parks, an African-American renaissance man who pulled himself out of rural poverty and the Jim Crow South to be a successful photographer, musician, composer, painter, writer, and film director. "Uncle Gordon," as he liked to be called, was most famous for two things: his photograph *American Gothic, Washington, DC*, which showed a black maid in front of an American flag in a federal building with a broom in one hand and a mop in the background, and for directing the first blaxploitation film, *Shaft*.

Teachings from the Bible, Buddhism, Taoism, and even *A Course in Miracles* became a focus of daily study and practice. It was a Unitarian Universalist Church that finally seemed like the right place to join for this period of broad exploration. In Unitarian Universalism, principles grounded in the humanistic teachings of all the world's religions are affirmed and promoted.

I also made a daily discipline of writing three pages every morning. At the end of my two years, I had filled seven journals of tiny handwritten notes in turquoise blue (which I believed was a color of healing) fountain pen ink. Halfway through my third notebook, about fifteen months into my "break" from the world of work, my daily writings started to be addressed directly to God. In that first entry to God, I confessed my fears and doubts about what I was doing. "Is this how madness starts? Am I still a part of you? Why can't I hear what your will is for me?" You'd think I might have given up the search at that time, but I kept on looking for answers.

I can't seem to find what I'm supposed to do with myself. I'm jumping around with no clear direction. One moment, I think I should be a graphic designer. Then I think I should go back to New York and work on prison reform. Or open a day care program or go to people's homes as a pet sitter. I even thought about starting a nonsexual escort service.

Those are all about how to cling to your possession of material things. The other things you are exploring may be more important.

More important than knowing how I'll cover my rent and pay for food and clothes?

Yes, if you're truly seeking how to live, not just earn a living.

But I have to earn a living.

Eventually, maybe. But if you are patient and keep listening, you may still learn something valuable.

I don't think I can wait.

The ads were everywhere. "Make money working at home." I saw them when I watched daytime TV. They were in the Help Wanted section of the paper and up at all the supermarkets. Wasn't this exactly what I was looking for? I could stay at home and take care of Caroline and still make money. The first ad I responded to got me a book for $49.95 providing lots of information on kinds of jobs you could do from home—medical or legal transcription, product reviewers, making sales calls, putting together fabric totes, and tips for finding these jobs. There was nothing really useful in the book, though it insisted that any failure to make money from the information it provided would be because I wasn't trying hard enough. One ad got me instructions on how to send out twenty chain letters requesting the recipients to send you back a dollar and send out twenty more letters themselves. Wasn't that called a pyramid scam?

The one scheme I put the most hope in was one where you started your own business as a sales distributor for an herbal supplement company. They sold herbal products that were supposed to get you healthier and lose weight, which were both things I needed to do. I started taking the products myself and bit the bullet by purchasing cases of their supplements to sell to other people. I joined weekly conference calls to hear from top moneymakers in the business. These were all enthusiastic representatives of the company who shared their inspirational stories about how they went from being unemployed and buried in debt to earning hundreds of thousands of dollars once they focused on building their businesses. But after months of trying to sell the products with the boxes still stacked in my office, I started to get a clearer picture of the business model. It wasn't really about selling the products. All those top earners didn't get their income and success from selling the most products. The way they were making their income was by recruiting new "distributors"—more desperate people like me who were looking for an alternative to nine-to-five employment with a regular employer.

This is even worse than if I had just sat around on my ass. Now all I've done is run up my credit card bill with useless products that I'm never going to sell. And I wouldn't even want to sell them because they don't work.

Didn't I warn you about being patient?

But I thought I had to take action. I really didn't imagine that trying to do something to make money would end up being worse for me than doing nothing.

Your instinct should have told you something. Remember that fortune cookie?

You mean, "If it sounds too good to be true, it probably is"? Maybe I should have known better. I just wanted so badly to find an answer to how I could make money. And they made it sound so easy.

Why do you think it should be easy?

You mean like Buddha said, "Life is suffering"?

Yes, Buddha comforted me. I never had any possessions of my own. I never had control over my life. But by accepting that life is suffering and not clinging to a desire for possessions or an easy life, I never needed to complain. What does your Bible say? Is it very different?

I don't know. Maybe not so different. In the Garden of Eden story,[15] *after Eve and Adam ate the fruit of knowledge of good and evil, as punishment, God told Eve that her pain would be increased in childbirth and that her desire would be for her husband and he would rule over her.*

And the punishment for the man?

God told Adam that he would have to toil in the ground that would be cursed with thorns and thistles until he returned to the ground.

Does that sound easy?

---

[15]   Genesis 2–3.

No, it doesn't.

Then maybe you should stop looking for "easy."

Even though money was still tight, once I stopped trying to make a quick buck, everything seemed clearer and I worried less. Perhaps it was true that anything worth doing ("creating," "growing," or "birthing") would have to take hard work and usually some amount of pain. Even relationships. God told Eve that her desire would be for Adam and that he would rule over her. It's not that I bought into the sexist aspect of the pronouncement but rather took it as a statement on human relationships. Those would take hard work too and often be painful. But was life suffering, as Buddha said?

Or was it like my mother's visions during childbirth? She had told me once when I was in middle school that she had a vision both times she gave birth to my brother and me. She said a Jainist once told her that every child was born with the meaning of life whispered to them. And because of her strong connections to my brother and me, she was somehow allowed to overhear the message. Both times, she said, she was flown up far above the earth to learn that meaning but, with each step as she descended back to her body, she would travel half the distance and lose half of the knowledge. It was a very mathematical vision, perfect for a physicist, based on Zeno's dichotomy paradox. The paradox says you can never reach your destination by splitting your distance in half. She would never completely lose the knowledge either but come close. After my brother was born, my mother said she couldn't remember anything about the vision, hadn't even remembered she had it. But when I was born, she remembered thinking, "Oh, here it is again." Still she couldn't recall the vision itself. It all came back to her, though, one day when she saw my hamster running in its wheel. That's what she learned when she floated above the earth! In her elevated position, she could see that everyone was just running around on earth like on a hamster wheel, going nowhere. Could that be the meaning of life? No wonder my mother was so cynical and always expected the worst to happen. Right then, I needed to avoid my mother. Her nature would only allow her to see a disastrous future for me from all this. My father's big life disappointment echoed in my mind. He always regretted being forced to dissolve his business only months before his position in the market would have made him millions, if only my mother had agreed to let him use our house as collateral to cover his investment. But my mother refused. She could only imagine losing everything, not that my father's gamble could pay off. She wouldn't be able to believe in what I was trying to do either.

To pay my bills, I continued to take advances from my credit cards. I also made small amounts of money pet sitting and dog walking, but spent the rest of my time writing and doing volunteer work. My new church supported a voluntary hospice program. I had spent a lot of time and energy trying to avoid thoughts of death but it was always there, just beneath the surface. It seemed that it was time to face it head-on and see if I could break its hold on me.

There was something about the loss or potential loss of someone that always drew me in. Wasn't I most drawn to stories where someone loses their life? Didn't I fall in love with all the characters that died? Wasn't I obsessed with the characters that died in *Torch Song Trilogy*, *Philadelphia*, *Into the Woods*, and *Forrest Gump?* Didn't I even fall for Jesus in *Jesus Christ Superstar?* Did I choose Caroline because she might die? I would watch a movie like *Long Time Companion* and find myself convulsing in tears and uncontrollable grief as Bruce Davison tells his lover dying from AIDS that it's okay for him to go. I was obsessed with death; I thought about it all the time. On the rare occasions when I used marijuana I would have a recurring bad trip focused on questions about death—mine and everyone else's in my life—eerily like the narrator's experience in Tolstoy's short story "The Memoirs of a Madman." Maybe if I approached it head-on by getting involved with a hospice program, I could get a better handle on death.

The hospice volunteer training program was powerful. It was a five-day curriculum that looked at the emotional, spiritual, and physical aspects of death. Participants shared their own moving personal experiences with death and grief. We heard from clergy, health care providers, and experienced volunteers. A nurse described to us what we could expect when the time draws near, including the "death rattle" that often results from an accumulation of fluids in the throat and upper chest of a person nearing death. It was explained to us that people who request services from the hospice program, as a nonmedical voluntary hospice, do not necessarily have to have a prognosis of six months or less, nor are they expected to forego all curative treatments. However, most had come to the point of accepting that death was both imminent and inevitable. We were also taught about the process of grief. In those five days, I learned so much more about the five stages of grief—denial, anger, bargaining, depression, and acceptance—than I had gotten from Bob Fosse's *All That Jazz*, which I'd seen about a hundred times when I worked as a movie theater usher at age seventeen. We were told not to expect from the family members a set pattern, intensity, or order for the stages of their grief. It was also important to remember that we would not be able to save them from their grief or fix anything for them. Our job would be to simply be there for them; to listen and be a source of support. We could provide assistance with household tasks, respite care when family members needed a break, and drive them to appointments. But this work was not about heroics. It was about having the honor of being with the dying and their loved ones during this sacred time in the cycle of life.

This intensive crash course in everything about death and grief was mysteriously comforting. While I usually felt like an emotional train wreck whenever I was confronted with death and grief, I was strangely composed throughout and after the hospice volunteer training. After completing the course, I was assigned around a dozen cases over the course of a year that were all heartbreaking but unexpectedly fortifying.

I spent a few months visiting Mariana, a devout Catholic at the end stages of cancer. Mariana lived in a tiny town house in Gaithersburg, Maryland, overflowing with religious artifacts. Throughout her lovely home, she had numerous crucifixes with the suffering Jesus, prayer candles, some golden painted icons of Jesus and her favorite saints, a shrine to the Virgin Mary, and a dozen different types of rosary beads that hung from lamps, book cases, statues, and anywhere else that would hold her decorative, meaningful necklaces. When I would visit her, she would ask me to pray with her—not for healing or to take away her pain. Her prayers were always of gratitude for the beautiful life she lived, the beautiful children and grandchildren she had in her life, and for the gift of God's love. She even thanked God for her cancer, saying it made her appreciate her life so much more. It reminded me of a line from the film *Shadowlands*, which chronicled love and loss in the life of author and theologian C.S. Lewis, "The pain now is part of the happiness then."[16]

Mariana's funeral was standing room only, filled with loved ones, friends, members of her church, and every medical and other service provider who met her during her illness. She had touched so many lives. Speaker after speaker shared how her faith and goodness had inspired them—made them feel honored to be granted the gift of having known her. All the love and gratitude that permeated the service made me feel uplifted rather than sad. It was only the speech by the priest that brought

---

[16]   Anthony Hopkins et al., *Shadowlands* (New York: HBO Home Video, 1998).

me down. He said that death wasn't originally God's plan for humanity in the Garden of Eden. But it was because of man's sin that death was brought into our world. What an uninspiring message!

It's hard for me to understand how Mariana was so accepting of her own death. She has such strong faith, I'm surprised she never asked God for a miracle to cure her.

Why would she? She felt her life was miracle enough.

And I really hated what that priest had to say. Why bring up sin, when Mariana's life was all about faith and goodness?

What wasn't true about what he said of the garden story?

Well God said if they ate the fruit, they would surely die. But instead they gained the knowledge of good and evil.[17]

But you said God punished them for their act, right?

Well, he sent them "East of Eden" so that they couldn't eat from the tree of life and live forever.

So doesn't that mean that the priest was right according to this story? It was their sin, what you thought was their first mistake, that introduced them to death.

True to the story, maybe. I just don't understand what we're supposed to learn from it. I don't see what the connection is between sin and death.

Maybe not between sin and death. Maybe the connection is between consciousness and death.

How are they connected?

Don't people live their lives differently because they know they will die?

---

[17] Genesis 2–3.

I guess if you're like Mariana, it can make you appreciate your life more. And if you believe in God's judgment at death, maybe you'll want to live your life more righteously.

So the garden story is about God's judgment?

Not really. By eating the fruit, Adam and Eve were able to distinguish between good and evil for themselves. So, I guess you could call that consciousness too. I suppose if you want your life to have meaning, you might want to use your conscience to choose to do more good than evil.

So maybe the priest had a point.

Another case I was assigned to was with an Eastern European family whose child was born more than three months premature, weighing less than two pounds. The baby was born without a fully formed skull, brain, or lungs. It was, medically, almost inconceivable that the baby was still alive and able to be brought home. The hospital had concluded that it was useless to attempt any more life-saving treatments. But despite the withdrawal of medical intervention, the baby did not die. So, they told the family to bring the baby home to die. It only took a few days—a few agonizing days. I bore witness to the family's misery as they endured the unimaginable sorrow of watching this helpless creature, which before his birth had represented their greatest hope and joy, lose his struggle for life. What sense could they make of this pain? I understood and shared their questions about what kind of God could allow this kind of senseless suffering.

This one is really hard to take. Why would God let this happen?

Does the suffering comes from God?

I'm not sure where I think it comes from. I remember after Dr. Coffin lost his twenty-three-year old son when his son's car crashed into the Boston Harbor, how Dr. Coffin reacted to a quiche-bearing, well-meaning visitor who said, "I just don't understand the will of God." He screamed back at her, "I'll say you don't, lady!"[18] *Dr. Coffin said that it is never the will of God when someone dies unnaturally. And Rabbi Harold Kushner, who lost his son at fourteen from a senseless genetic disease of premature aging, believed that God could either be good and loving or be all-powerful, but not both. Rabbi Kushner said he preferred to believe in a God that's good and loving.*[19] *I'd like to too.*

Then why do you still ask that question?

I was assigned to Catherine, who was deeply faithful and prayed to God to keep her alive so she could go on taking care of the two developmentally disabled boys whom she had adopted from Haiti. She had emigrated from France to marry more than twenty years earlier but had divorced her husband several years before I met her, and before she was able to get her citizenship. Her ex-husband, with a new family of his own, wanted nothing to do with the two boys, now age nineteen and twenty-one, though they had adopted them together during their marriage. He didn't see it as any of his responsibility to care for these adopted boys and had no sympathy for Catherine's anguish as she considered their fate once she was gone. The sons had not earned US citizenship either, so they were not eligible for any governmental assistance. If she were to die now, her sons would become homeless and have no one to support them—maybe even be deported back to Haiti.

Of all my clients in the hospice program, I grew closest to Catherine. I would spend hours with her each week at her cozy two-bedroom

---

[18] William Sloane Coffin, "Alex's Death, January 23, 1983" in *Collected Sermons of William Sloane Coffin, The Riverside Years,* vol. 2 (Louisville: Westminster John Knox Press, 2008).

[19] Harold Hushner, *When Bad Things Happen to Good People* (New York: Random House Inc, 1981).

apartment in Gaithersburg, Maryland. She shared with me her fears about leaving behind her sons. I listened to her disappointment that all the generosity and love with which she lived her life didn't get rewarded with a better outcome for her and those she loved. She believed in the power of prayer and in miracles. To some extent it was a miracle that she was still alive, since the prognosis of her rare condition, which was turning her internal organs into stone, should have killed her at least a year earlier. But she felt that she still had too much left to do. We would sit around the small table in her eat-in kitchen, scheming about helping her sons.

The boys, not biologically related to each other, had been living on the streets of Haiti after each had lost both parents to AIDS. Catherine and her husband met the boys as beggars during a day-trip to Haiti while vacationing in the Dominican Republic. She couldn't get the pathetic young orphan boys out of her mind and made it her mission to adopt them. Now, both boys were over six feet tall with dark, handsome faces and full heads of mini dreadlocks. They bore no resemblance to their mother, Catherine, who stood only five feet tall and was pale and stocky with wavy light brown hair. The younger boy was still in high school, having been held back a few times due to his learning disability. The older boy worked a few hours a week for minimum wage at a fast food restaurant. The two of them would have a difficult time surviving without Catherine. But I knew a little about advocacy, political and legal. There were politicians who would care about Catherine's and her boys' plights. As talented athletes, both boys had participated and done well in the Special Olympics. Its founder, Eunice Kennedy Shriver, and her family still had a lot of juice in government. A few calls to the right people connected to the Special Olympics and members of the Kennedy-Shriver family did the trick. Before long, Catherine and both her boys were taking their oaths of citizenship. A strongly worded letter from an attorney to Catherine's deadbeat ex-husband was all it took to get the man to create a trust for the boys from all the years of child support he owed. Eventually, the boys were approved for Supplemental Security Income and Medicaid as well as Section 8 housing. Catherine cried both tears of joy and melancholy when her sons moved out to live in their own shared apartment in a program for developmentally disabled young adults, which their new government benefits enabled. She moved to a smaller one-bedroom apartment closer to me in Silver Spring. She and I still prayed together for her to be healed, but her heart was no longer in it.

Catherine is just as faithful and certainly is more deserving than Caroline and I are for a miracle. I think that's what's confusing me. If God is able to intervene, like when Caroline's life was saved—at least twice now—I don't get why God would ever choose not to.

You think it's God's choice? Didn't you say you thought that God was not all-powerful?

I don't really know what to think. I can't quite buy into everything that Rabbi Kushner believes. Because I've seen first hand that God can make miracles happen. So then I'm back to thinking that God must not be as loving as we'd like to believe. Because if God can answer prayers and heal the sick, then not to do it is kind of cruel.

Maybe God answered different prayers for Catherine. She wanted to live so her sons would be all right. And now they will, right?

Another case had me rushing to a family's home in the last hours of their loved one's life. The medical hospice had left the family to be on their own and they were freaking out. The man was lying in the small hospital bed with his eyes glazed and mouth ajar. The death rattle the nurse had warned us about in training was almost deafening. The man's family, his wife and adult son and daughter, stood in the corners of the room, as far away from the dying man as they could get without leaving the room. This was not peaceful, like when we had put my dog Caleb to sleep. The rattle sounded angry and went on for hours. I didn't know how to comfort the family and just had to fake it. I pretended the noise wasn't disturbing and sat in a chair quietly next to the man as he died. I asked if they wanted to tell me anything about his life and they did. We were all holding hands, sitting around his bed, smiling quietly when he finally stopped breathing.

So, what is it, Sya Meh, that attracts you to the dying? Do you feel that a person's death makes them somehow more dear?

I'm not sure. I guess the loss or threat of loss sometimes makes you appreciate someone's life more. But just because someone's dying doesn't automatically make a person more valueable. I visited the wife of one patient who was a mean, miserable man before he got sick and he was still a mean, miserable man while he was dying. That's probably an exception though. Generally, I think, being conscious of death makes you realize just how precious life is.

Would you be with Caroline if she was not dying?

That's kind of a rude question, Ah Kung.

Why? Will you not answer it?

I'd like to think I'm with Caroline despite the fact that she was dying. Certainly not because of it.

Nothing romantic about loving a dying person? Nothing about wanting to save her life?

I mean obviously I've wanted her life to be saved. But I hope there's more to it than that. Otherwise, there wouldn't be much to our relationship if she got better and lived.

The money finally ran out in earnest, about two months into what would have been my third year without earning an income. The writing came to nothing. Most of my moneymaking schemes ended up costing me well more than I earned from them. I maxed out all my credit cards and borrowed as much as I could from every family member I dared. As personally enriching as the voluntary hospice work had been, there didn't seem much prospect for me to transition my voluntary work to anything where I could earn a living.

I resigned myself to going to a temp agency to place me with office work just to make a little money. The second job I got with the temp agency was with the small biotech company typing up standard operating procedures to replace lost electronic files. It was steady work that I could do at home for a pretty decent hourly wage. Within a month, they asked me to work for them full-time as a senior document control specialist for more than I made heading up programs at the nonprofit, and with better benefits. When Ken resigned as my manager, less than a year later, I knew I was well on my way to a new career—one that before long could more than make up for all the time I had taken off.

I'm so glad that time's over. Now I can get back to taking care of Caroline and the dogs.

There is more than one way to care for others, no? I'd like to think that I cared for your family, even if I never paid the bills.

Of course. But it's not like we can live off of Caroline's Social Security. So at this point I've got to figure out how to pay our bills.

Did you learn what you hoped about death?

Maybe. It's kind of ironic, you know. The more I was around dying people, the more I felt that Caroline was not going to die. It's hard to believe it now, after all she went through, but I think she's actually going to beat AIDS. When we lost Stephen, it really brought home just how lucky Caroline is to still be alive. A third miracle maybe!

So not a waste of time?

No, not a complete waste. But it will be good to be able to go back and focus on work and my career again.

Funny. That's one thing your hospice patients never talked about.

Well, I feel pretty lucky that I'm able to start a whole new good career after this kind of break. Maybe this is what God had in mind for me all along.

I guess we shall see, Sya Meh.

CHAPTER 17

East of Eden
(My Last Mistake)

Of all my conversations with Ah Kung, the one we never had was about the night he died right under my hands. Ah Kung had helped me get through so much in my life but now, it seemed, he was the one causing my problems. Things had gotten so bad for me that I felt my only option was to walk away from my job... again. This time, I might be completely letting go of the career I had spent twenty years building—one that had given me more security, success, and material wealth than I had dreamed possible: everything I thought I wanted for Caroline and our family. But I was falling apart and I had to get out.

Just a year earlier, everything had been different. Then, I was considered an effective leader at one of the most successful and respected biopharmaceutical companies in the San Francisco Bay Area. I felt proud that I was able to make a great living working for a company that helped save lives. It even turned out that this was the very company that had developed two of the three drugs from Caroline's initial experimental HIV drug cocktail, including the world's first protease inhibitor, which had saved her life twenty years earlier. I had a great office on the top floor of my building, as close to the corner as existed, with an amazing view of the bay. My team of twelve, which had quadrupled in size in just four years, had been happy. Based on their nomination, I had even been honored with a Great Manager award at the end-of-year celebration for our organization. My boss had considered me a top performer on his team and held me up as a model for positive employee engagement.

A year before all my problems, Caroline and I were able to get legally married, twenty-three years and one week from the day of our blessed union. The ceremony was held in our small progressive Christian church in the Twin Peaks section of San Francisco, presided over by our lesbian senior minister whom we considered a friend. While we recited the same vows (except for my "not even death" line) from our blessed union more than two decades earlier, this legal wedding was very different. This time both my parents attended and my father walked me down the aisle. Caroline's brother J.D., whose past abuse could only have been forgiven by someone as generous and loving as Caroline, flew in from Oklahoma to fill in for Caroline's late father to "give her away." Our dogs figured prominently in the ceremony: our foxhound mix Harley was the flower girl, and our springer spaniels Taylor and Rocky were the ring bearers. We hired the musical director and professional singers from our church's music program to perform the songs: Carole King's "Will You Love Me Tomorrow?," the Beatles' "In My Life" (a repeat from our 1991 blessed union), and "Over the Rainbow/What a Wonderful World" as performed by Israel "IZ" Kamakawiwo'ole. Members of my extended family, colleagues from my work and our lives in San Francisco, as well as fellow parishioners from our church attended as guests. We had a well-catered reception in the church's social hall for all the wedding guests, followed up with a wilder after-party for the younger crowd. All but one of my staff members came to the celebration (both the marriage ceremony and the after-party). I was incredibly touched when one of my team members told me it was the most beautiful wedding she had ever attended.

But something had gone terribly wrong. I now had a new boss, my ninth in eight years at the company. She didn't like or trust me. Half my team had started to turn against me. I knew that I was completely losing it when my executive coach, Nastasya, a woman I had hired and my company paid a pretty penny for to help me gain more "executive presence," asked me a question and I completely broke down sobbing. I had cried the first time we met as well, when I was supposed to be interviewing her. In the interview, Nastasya asked me, "So what's going on with you?" and I started tearing up. I broke down sharing with her that my new boss was pressuring me to reorganize my team and I believed it would mean some of them would end up losing their jobs. Five years earlier, I had been forced to lay off half my staff. My boss at that time had asked me to pick two of my four staff members to be targeted for a layoff. For months, I had to interact with them every day, acting like I didn't know anything about what was coming. I cried every night and barely slept while I held the secret. But I had gotten through it and was even rewarded with a promotion a few months later. I didn't think I could live through that again, not with my current team members, about whom I cared so much now—people who had come to my wedding. My coach Nastasya was sympathetic and supportive. She had a gentle and benevolent spirit that was in keeping with how I imagined she would be from her résumé. Her profile showed her previous occupation as a Buddhist scholar and college professor. She had taught Buddhism at both of my alma maters in New York and I sensed we would have a connection even before we met. Something about Nastasya's aura allowed me to feel safe enough to open up to her and share what was weighing on my heart. We had met four times by then, and I had found myself tearing up a little every time. But this time, the tears were not just slipping out. This was an all-out psychic collapse.

"How would it be for you if you just did your best and you couldn't protect anyone?" Nastasya asked.

My whole body was shaking. I couldn't talk. Couldn't breathe.

"Breathe... breathe... breathe," Nastasya urged. With my eyes closed, I could hear Nastasya demonstrating the deep breaths she wanted me to take.

Though it was ultimately a losing battle, Nastasya had done her best during our coaching sessions to help me try to recognize when I was driving too hard and was too much on a mission for the people around me. She gave me daily practices as homework between our meetings. They were unconventional practices, hardly what one would expect from a business executive coach. One of the daily assignments was to bring to mind those loved ones who mattered most to me and to notice the emotions and sensations that arose in my body as I brought them to mind. One morning I found myself thinking about my brother, Martin, and feeling a terrible sadness that I had lost him as my best friend after the birth of his son, Leonardo.

It had happened years earlier, when Leonardo was a little over two months old and I stopped Martin and his wife Pamela from taking Leonardo on a plane trip. They were all planning to fly out to Ohio for the confirmation ceremony into the Catholic church of Pamela's nephew and godson. My parents were beside themselves with worry for Leonardo's welfare. The family of Pamela's sister had not yet met Leonardo, and Pamela and Martin were excited to make the trip. But right around that time, rather hysterical reports were all over the news about a new pandemic of swine flu, which had made its way into Mexico, and officials feared it could spread in the United States. The European Union health commissioner had already advised Europeans to postpone nonessential travel to the United States and Mexico. My parents begged Martin and Pamela to cancel their trip, showing them articles about how children under two years old were the most vulnerable to the pandemic. And everyone knew that the surest way to catch something is from the recirculated air in crowded airplanes. But the new parents had consulted with several doctors and were convinced that there was no real danger. Since my brother and I were so close, my parents hoped I could change his mind.

I sided with my parents. Even though there were already a few voices that were starting to say that the cries of pandemic were an exaggeration, I thought, why take the chance? I couldn't help thinking about my mother's little sister who died after my grandmother refused to heed her uncle's warning. Her uncle had warned that something terrible would happen if my grandmother traveled across China with her baby. And my mother's little sister died. Leonardo was like a miracle to all of us. My parents had nearly given up hope of ever having a grandchild. When Leonardo was born, so perfect, to Pamela who had just turned forty and Martin, already forty-six, it brought us all indescribable joy. How could I risk even the remotest possibility of Leonardo's catching swine flu? I called Martin and told him I couldn't fathom how he could consider taking such a senseless risk. When he insisted that he and Pamela knew what they were doing, I told him I thought he was being pussy-whipped by his wife. Then I wrote an email to Pamela's sister, urging her to tell Pamela she wouldn't hold it against her if they didn't make the trip. Pamela's sister told Pamela about my email. They cancelled the trip. But my brother never forgave me for my interference, or maybe for the name I called him. I tried convincing myself that I had done the right thing. Protecting Leonardo was more important than my relationship with my brother. But now all I could feel was the heartbreaking loss of my best friend.

I'm having such a hard time these days with this feeling that I always have to save everybody. It's really starting to hurt me.

Maybe it's because you can't.

But that's not true. Look at Caroline! How many times has her life been saved? How can you say I can't ever save anyone?

Not that you can't ever. That you can't <u>always</u>.

*   *   *

When the judge took his seat in chambers, I knew he was going to rule against us. After all the money I had spent on legal expenses, private investigators, and expert witness fees over three court hearings, we were going to lose. There was little consolation in the judge's final pronouncement that "the conduct of the defendant trustees during the decedent's last illness, death, and funeral was ill-advised, insensitive, and despicable." As our lawyer pointed out, in some ways that made it even worse. How could the judge find that the defendants were despicable, but not hostile enough to have them removed as trustees? It seemed inconceivable that I could have fought so hard and spent so much time, energy, and money for us to lose in the end. Maybe I should have known better. The court was in Oklahoma, after all. This was a state where the judge we had the misfortune of drawing in our first two hearings was famous throughout the country for denying a transgender person a name change—TWICE. The second time was after his first ruling had already been reversed by the appellate court. So when he did it a second time, many felt like it was just out of pure bigotry and a sense that he was above the law.

I had hoped that our luck was going to turn, though. That first infamous judge, who had already ruled against us after our first two hearings, had withdrawn from our case, supposedly due to a schedule conflict. It seemed obvious that he preferred not to preside over our case, once our attorneys had filed a motion asking the judge to recuse himself due to his bias against homosexuals. He denied the motion but mysteriously came up with a scheduling conflict a month before our final trial date. Unfortunately, the new judge didn't make any difference in the final outcome. All the fighting I did, all the money I spent, all the prayers I offered up to God weren't enough to protect Caroline and her brother from their "despicable" cousins.

The "ill-advised, insensitive, and despicable" conduct the judge referenced started right after the death of Caroline's father Todd. Caroline had been alone with her father, holding his hand at the moment he passed away. She texted me the news, just before I boarded the plane to join her in Oklahoma. Then Caroline's Aunt Mitsy—Todd's baby sister—called. Caroline was sharing her grief with her aunt when the "despicable" defendants entered the room. Caroline's cousin Susy and Aunt Lucile, Susy's mother and the oldest living sibling of Caroline's father, couldn't stand Mitsy. Lucile told Susy she wanted Caroline out of the room.

Susy obliged by demanding, "Caroline, go out in the hallway and make your calls."

"Who do you think you are, Jesus, Mary, and Joseph?" Caroline fumed. She stood very close to Susy and her paralyzed right arm was shaking out of control from her anger and grief.

Susy answered, "I'll tell you who! I was his power of attorney. I'm his executor and his trustee. And if you don't leave, I'm going to get security."

Before the exchange got any more heated, Todd's best friend arrived and comforted Caroline out in the hallway, leaving Caroline's kin to be alone with Todd's body.

Susy Cooper and her husband R.J. had convinced Caroline's father and mother in 2002 to name them as successor trustees for the special needs trust, for which Caroline and her brother were the beneficiaries.

The trust had originally been drawn up in 1996, at a time when both Caroline and her brother J.D., who also turned out to be gay, had tested positive for HIV. Caroline's mother Dee wanted a special needs trust for Caroline and J.D., so they could benefit from the sizable estate without jeopardizing their eligibility for government assistance like Supplemental Security Income and Medicaid. Caroline was already on both programs at the time the trust was created. J.D. wasn't receiving government assistance but, in 1996, HIV and AIDS were still a death sentence and chances were that someday he would. When the Coopers found out about the trust in 2002 and how much it was worth, approximately $2 million, they insisted that they would be much better trustees than the banks that were originally to be appointed after both parents died. They were family, after all. And family does right by family. Besides, they argued, a bank would just charge them lots of money to administer the trust without ever really *caring* for Caroline and J.D.

The Coopers' first act as trustees, less than twenty-four hours after Todd's death, was to serve Caroline with an eviction notice from her family home. They handed it to Caroline as we were leaving her father's viewing at the funeral home. The notice dictated that Caroline and her guests were to vacate the property by nine the next morning, the morning of the funeral. The home, which the family had lived in since the early 1950s, was located literally on a street called Memory Lane. It was the only home her parents had ever lived in during Caroline's lifetime and it held all their memories. Built in the 1930s, it was the largest home on the block with by far the most acreage. But it was not a fancy home. Only the minimum amount of maintenance was ever performed and it didn't look like any renovations or improvements had been made since before 1970. The home and surrounding property, which included a large shop, numerous outbuildings, and almost an acre and a half of land, were overflowing with everything Caroline's parents had collected over sixty years. Dee had been a collector of the things she loved: artwork, jewelry, sewing projects, family photographs, and decorative ornaments like Precious Moments. Todd had collected what he loved: mechanical equipment, tools, scrap metal, motorcycles and cars (in various stages of repair), and firearms. When Todd went into the hospital for the last time, he told Caroline, as she always did when she visited, to stay at the family home. That didn't matter to the trustees.

"We have an eviction notice for J.D. too. If he had bothered to come to the viewing, we'd have given it to him." Susy's voice was cool and measured, like she had been rehearsing this scene every day for the decade that had passed since she had gotten herself appointed as trustee.

Caroline was so hot that the single-digit temperatures of that December evening in Oklahoma couldn't keep her in the same room. She nearly lost her balance as she pushed through the door to the frosty outside air.

"How can you do this?" I asked them.

"We're the trustees, and the home is now the property of the trust."

"But Caroline and J.D. are the beneficiaries of the trust!"

"No, they're not."

"What do you mean? Who is?"

"Some charities: the family's Baptist church in Alabama and a couple of medical clinics. Look, don't leave Caroline alone outside in the cold. This is just the way it has to be."

I didn't want to leave Caroline alone in the cold, so I did go out to her. But there was no way that I was just going to let it be that way. If Susy and R.J. thought they could pretend that Caroline and J.D. were not the beneficiaries and they could do whatever they wanted with everything in the estate, they were mistaken. Or were they?

Ultimately, with the judge's final ruling, the trustees were determined to have "sole and absolute discretion" over the assets of the trust and any distributions made to or for the benefit of the beneficiaries. The court was not swayed by the testimony of our expert witness, that the trust's 160-acre estate in Colorado should have been valued at nearly twice the $290,000 sale price the trustees sold it for. It wasn't important that, three months before he died, Todd had given Caroline the keys to the Colorado property on her fiftieth birthday, saying, "The place is yours now, baby." The court didn't care that the trustees ignored the expressed wishes of Dee, clearly specified in her trust, that she never wanted to be placed in a nursing home. Instead, the Coopers took the opportunity, when Dee screamed to her husband, "If you don't get these vultures out of my home, I'm going to kill myself," to have her committed to a mental hospital and placed on suicide watch for eleven days. It was easy enough for them to get her locked away in a nursing home from there, where she died of a broken heart only six months later. If Dee, who was only suffering from the earliest stages of Alzheimer's, had been allowed to stay at home, she surely would have outlived Todd. If she had lived, she could have removed the "vultures" as trustees, like she tried to do four years before her death, until her husband vetoed the move. We presented evidence that the trustees raided Todd's safe deposit box and home safe two days before he died. Our witnesses testified about tens of thousands of dollars in cash and fifty ounces of gold that never materialized after their raids. We showed that the trustees had kept for themselves a $500 refund check from a service they chose to cancel from Todd's prearranged and prepaid funeral expenses. We argued that the auction of all Todd's business assets amounted to little more than a fire sale, with thousands of valuable items being sold off as "scrap metal" or "junk." We presented all the incidents of blatant hostility of the trustees towards Caroline and J.D.: the eviction notices, ordering the funeral home prevent the children from having copies of their father's death certificate, denying medical and service dog training expenses for Todd's dog Rocky, who Caroline adopted at Todd's request, refusing to reimburse the children for an obituary for their father, refusing to let them have any of the vehicles, refusing to purchase a hot water heater for J.D. so he had to live through a winter of single-digit temperatures in a home with no heat, refusing to honor the document J.D. had signed appointing me his power of attorney, refusing to give Caroline a cent of reimbursement for the wedding expenses of Todd and Dee's only daughter. I testified that the perfect strangers who bought the family home (also probably for less than what it was really worth), showed more compassion to Caroline and J.D. by letting them tour the home, from which the trustees had previously locked them out. According to the court, all these things were immaterial under Oklahoma law.

On the morning of Todd's funeral, I called the trustees and told them that, if they wanted Caroline evicted, they would have to call the sheriff to do it. The sheriff never arrived. A few days after the funeral, the trustees realized I was not going to let them get away without a reading of the trust. The reading affirmed that Caroline and J.D. were indeed the lifetime beneficiaries and that the purpose of the trust was for their lives to "be enriched and made more enjoyable and comfortable." It would also show that Caroline and J.D. were entitled to all the "tangible personal property" of the estate, without any interference by the trustees, and the children needed to have access to the home in order to separate the property between them. Caroline and J.D. were able to get most of what had the greatest sentimental value to them. But all the legal action I had funded was a total loss. The final ruling was issued about two months before I hired Nastasya as my coach.

Taking up that fight was a really costly lesson—emotionally and financially. I truly believed since they were in the wrong, we couldn't possibly lose. I thought that right would have to win out over wrong—good would always win out over evil. It's hard to accept that the world doesn't work that way.

This is nothing new. Outcomes are often dictated by other than what's right. In this case, it was the biases of Caroline's home state.

But that's not how the world should work! Good has to win out over evil, doesn't it?

Eventually, maybe. Wasn't there a great civil rights leader who said something about this topic?

Sure, Martin Luther King Jr. said, "The arc of the moral universe is long, but it bends towards justice."[20] Is that supposed to be comforting?

It might be some comfort to consider that the cost to him was far more dear than yours. You still have the opportunity to learn something from it.

What am I supposed to learn? That life is unfair? That I've got to take the good with the bad? That's a pretty depressing lesson. And how do I reconcile it, when I believe one thing is right and others are just as convinced that the opposite is right? Take marriage equality. I'm sure that gays and lesbians should be able to make a legal commitment to each other. And they should be able to make that commitment before God and the state. To me, that's a matter of fairness and justice. It's something that reflects a moral universe. But there are many others, like the legislators in Oklahoma and clearly Susy and R.J., who are just as convinced that gay marriage goes against God. Only one perspective can be right. How do I know I'm right and not them?

---

20   Martin Luther King Jr., "How Long, Not Long" (speech, Montgomery, Alabama, March 25, 1965).

You don't. But that you're willing to ask the question is a good sign. It means you are willing to question your beliefs, not just accept something told to you. What are your reasons for believing as you do?

It's because I feel that God as well as nature favors diversity and being compassionate and just to one another. So something like gay marriage, which reflects our human diversity as well as compassion and justice, seems right, not wrong.

And its opponents? Why do they believe as they do?

Usually, they just argue that it goes against God as written in the Bible. Leviticus does tell Moses that he "shall not lie with a male as with a woman; it is an abomination."²¹ But the word "abomination" shows up four other times in Leviticus about eating leftovers and certain "unclean" types of animals. And I don't see those people getting all worked up about the other 612 rules in Leviticus. Most of those rules just helped protect the health and hygiene of people living in the time it was written. In today's era of refrigeration, modern medicine, and cleaning agents, I doubt anyone references Leviticus for rules to live by other than the one against homosexuality.

Then be content with your position, especially as more and more people are coming around to it.

Yeah, it's pretty amazing that marriage equality has now become the law of the land. We were all literally dancing in the streets at gay pride after that ruling came down from the Supreme Court. But then less than a year later, we saw our country's biggest mass murder of gay people at a night club in Orlando. So it's hard to feel safe. People like Susy and R.J. will always think they're better than anyone who's gay. And there's nothing I can do about it!

Except pray for them.

---

²¹   Leviticus 18:22.

About two months after I lost the court case, I also lost my church. I knew it had happened when Magda's eyes pierced through me from across the table. The way she was looking at me felt like she wanted to put her hands around my neck and squeeze. Magda was going to be our new interim pastor. Though I was the president of the church council, it had out-voted me and selected Magda. I had agreed to take on the role of council president after our senior minister, Sharon, had been pushed out. Officially, Sharon retired. But it was only after several members of the congregation, led by Magda and another council member, Laura, made it clear they wanted Sharon gone. I had written a letter to the council in support of Sharon. I knew our pastor was having some health problems and I believed the death of several older members of the congregation in the last year had taken a toll on her spirit. The congregation only had about twenty active members. I suggested we ought to have an open dialogue with Sharon. If she wasn't meeting our expectations, much of that blame needed to fall on us for not being clear about what our expectations were. Everyone was too polite to tell her to her face when they felt let down by her. But complaining about her behind her back was a different story.

It was after we learned that Sharon was going to retire that Caroline and I decided to get legally married. We wanted our pastor, whom we had gotten to know and care for socially in four years of attending this church, to marry us. She had made her decision to retire while Caroline and I were out of town for eight weeks, on our eight thousand mile, cross-country sabbatical road trip (with three service dogs in tow) that went from San Francisco to New York. The trip spanned from as far north as Montana and as far south as New Orleans, and had us visiting sights, friends, and relatives in Nevada, Utah, Wyoming, Colorado, Texas, Alabama, Georgia, North Carolina, West Virginia, Maryland, Delaware, New Jersey, New York, and Vermont. I had sent my letter to the council while on the road, but it didn't make any difference. The forces against Sharon were already too strong. She married us in August and was gone by the end of October.

In such a small congregation, everyone who shows up on a regular basis can expect to find themselves asked to volunteer for something or another at every turn. The same ten people served as ushers, liturgists, coffee hour hosts, and council and committee members. I wasn't surprised when the council president asked me if I would be on the interim minister search committee. I was a little surprised when the only candidate we were able to bring in for an interview told us that, if he were offered the job, he would not accept. He had read through our profile, heard the story of what had happened with the last minister, and saw how most of our budget was supported not through member pledges but instead from rental income from companies that used our spire as a cell phone tower and a school in the building we owned next door. He told us, "Your church is addicted to safety. Until your congregation is ready for change, no one can succeed in this role."

With no other options, we turned to two of our members who were pastors: Magda and Stewart. They were among the ten who were already involved in multiple church activities and committees. Stewart was one of my favorite people. I had been impressed by the powerful sermons he had delivered as a guest preacher. He and I had enjoyed many philosophical, political, and theological/spiritual conversations when we participated in Bible Study meetings and worked together on the church outreach committee. But there was something about Magda that I mistrusted. I knew that a good proportion of the ranting against Sharon had come from Magda, even though Sharon was the one who had sponsored Magda for her ministerial ordination. Magda always seemed dissatisfied and impatient. As head of the board of deacons, Magda was responsible for church hospitality activities and was also responsible for getting volunteers from the church to help with our wedding reception. When we briefly left the reception to go to Pastor Sharon's office to sign the wedding certificate, which must be filled out error-free or it has to be completely reissued, Magda barged into the office and told us we needed to cut the cake right then so the volunteers could go home. When the certificate was signed after we cut the cake and had our champagne toasts, Pastor Sharon and both of our witnesses made mistakes signing the document. We had to go back to the county clerk's office to purchase a new certificate and then had to run around to get it signed again for refiling. My mother had singled out Magda as the one person at our wedding who did not seem like a nice person. But the church was desperate to have some kind of pastoral leadership after Sharon's departure. The search committee's proposal was for Magda and Stewart to serve as temporary co-pastors for a period of six months, while we worked with the congregation to become more open to change. At the annual congregational meeting a month into their co-pastorate, I was affirmed by the congregation as the new president of the church council.

Before long, Magda and Laura, the other person who had been behind the campaign to push Sharon out, started complaining about Stewart. They ascribed to him many of the same flaws they had attributed to Sharon. Suddenly, the story was that Magda did everything. All Stewart ever did was work on his sermon every other week. So what if people appreciated Stewart's sermons, that they were intellectually and spiritually stimulating? It was just coincidence that, on weeks Stewart preached, there was nearly double the attendance compared to the number who attended when Magda preached. Magda proposed to the council to get rid of Stewart and for us to name her as the new official interim minister, to serve in that capacity on her own for the foreseeable future. On the council, only Laura was enthusiastic about Magda. But after an initial vote of 2-2, with one abstention, the council member who had abstained feared that another open search would be unsuccessful in hiring an outside interim minister. So she changed her vote in favor of hiring Magda.

After the vote, Don, my vice president on the council, asked me what they could do for me to make me okay with the vote. I couldn't say anything. All I could do was cry. I didn't know exactly why I was crying; what was happening to me. I felt like I was in mourning. No one had died but, somehow, I was experiencing a deep sense of grief—such an intense feeling of loss. Was it that I had failed to save my church? Failed to save Stewart? Tears kept pouring down my face as the rest of the council discussed how we should not tell Stewart until Magda officially accepted the "call." They strategized that the call letter should come from me, as the president of the council. Laura would draft the letter for my signature. The notification to Stewart, after everything was settled, should come from Don.

At my last council meeting, when I imagined that Magda would have liked to choke me if the table hadn't separated us, I was even more distraught. The meeting facilitator, a pastoral consultant hired by Laura, opened the meeting by asking everyone to share how he or she was feeling. By the time she got to me, I couldn't speak. I couldn't breathe. My whole body was shaking as I wept. It was all too much for me to feel I had failed everyone so miserably. I had to leave the room if I was ever going to find my breath again. When I gained a little composure and was able to return to my seat, that's when I thought Magda wanted to choke the life out of me. I only set foot in my church one more time after that day—for Stewart's last sermon.

I told my coach Nastasya about when I lost my church, since it was so similar to when I couldn't breathe during our coaching session. That's when I started to feel so out of control—so full of unspeakable grief. It really felt to me like someone was going to die and it would be my fault.

What was the point of the story about the soldier Nastasya told you?

It was a story about a soldier with PTSD—post-traumatic stress disorder. He kept robbing stores every Fourth of July with a toy gun because his best friend had been killed years earlier on the Fourth of July, and he had failed to save him. His PTSD made him like a broken record, stuck in a groove. It was forcing him to relive that incident every year on the same day with the subconscious hope of having another outcome. I think her point was that I was doing something similar

How was it similar?

She said when I take these actions to try to save someone else, I often sacrifice my own interests. I think she was hinting that makes me like that soldier. She said that, when I refuse to consider the cost to me while I'm on a mission to save someone else, it's a distortion. I did it with my brother. I did it with the lawsuit. I did it with my church. I did it when I went around my new boss to her peers and her boss to get their support so I wouldn't have to fire anyone from my team. I saved my team member by doing it, but I lost the trust of my new boss.

Do you think Nastasya's right? Do you think you are also stuck like the soldier?

Maybe. When I consider how, through my whole life, I have always wanted to be some kind of a savior, it is like I am repeating some scene.

Do you know what scene you're repeating?

I'm not sure.

Think about what Nastasya kept asking you to do: "Breathe... breathe... breathe..."

When you stopped breathing under my hands. I wasn't able to save you.

Why did you think I was supposed to be saved?

Because I loved you and should have been able to save you.

Your mistake was believing you could save me. You were nine. I was eighty-six with a heart condition. How could you save me?

That's just it. Since I couldn't save you, I keep trying to relive a scenario where I might be able to save someone else. For most of my life, that's what drove me and made most things possible for me. It's just in this past year that I kept failing at almost every attempt.

But why expect that of yourself? Didn't you say you accepted that even God is not all-powerful and can't always save everyone? What was it that your Dr. Coffin used to say about God?

That God gives us minimum protection, maximum support.

Do you imagine yourself greater than God?

Of course not. But I do believe in miracles.

Have you figured out how these miracles happen? You said before that, if it were through divine intervention, it would make God pretty cruel. And you still don't believe in a cruel God, do you?

No, but I think maybe I'm starting to make sense of it. I read something recently in a book called "The Heart of Christianity" by Marcus Borg that we studied in our spiritual conversations meetings at my new church. Borg said there's no such thing as divine intervention, but instead it's all about "divine intention" and "divine interaction."[22] God doesn't make miracles happen. People do, when they love one another as God loves us.

---

[22] Marcus J. Borg, *The Heart of Christianity: Rediscovering a Life of Faith* (New York: HarperOne, 1989).

All the miracles in my life have come through my interaction with other people, such as the faith healer in Brazil, the nurses and doctors at St. Vincent's, the researchers, drug developers and doctors who created new treatments for AIDS. Those people were demonstrating the intention of God—that we love and care for one another. It also goes with what the wonderful minister at my new church says all the time: "God has no hands but our hands; no feet but our feet…" I can now see that God may be powerless to prevent bad things from happening, but it's still possible to experience beautiful miracles sometimes through divine intention and divine interaction. It's no longer a contradiction for me. I have my new church to thank for that.

So though you lost a church, it seems like you found a home.

It really is kind of a mysterious blessing. I'd like to imagine the same might be possible for my work situation. I felt I had to leave my job because it had become unbearable. I felt such a responsibility to try to protect everyone. But in the end, I didn't protect anyone.

That's where you're wrong, Sya Meh. You did protect someone.

Who did I protect?

The nine-year-old child who blamed herself for not saving me. That's why you had to leave. You needed the time to forgive yourself.

But now I feel afraid. I thought my life had meaning because I was successful in my career and it allowed me to enjoy a comfortable life.

Was my life meaningless because I never achieved wealth and success?

Of course I didn't mean that. You're saying it should be like in the book we studied for the fall sermon series at my new church. In "The Road to Character," David Brooks wrote about needing to focus less on our resume virtues and more on our eulogy virtues.[23] I can see the value

---

[23] David Brooks, *The Road to Character* (New York: Random House, 2015).

in that. But what if giving up my job meant that I've screwed up my whole future?

The future is an illusion. There is only now.

So how will I know what I'm supposed to do now?

As you always have. Through your faith and judgment—everything you have learned through your life. And when the next thing you are meant to do comes along, do it.

But I'm afraid the road I'm on now is going to be a lot bumpier than before.

Perhaps. But perhaps that's not a bad thing. Perhaps it's like that garden story you are so fond of. Before they were sent East of Eden, the woman was told that giving birth would be painful and that she will always have desire for her spouse, but will never be able to feel secure about the relationship. And the man was told that he would have to toil to bring forth food from the ground until he is returned to it.

Yeah, those were their punishments for eating of the tree of knowledge of good and evil.

But what if they are not God's punishment, but instead God's gift?

I never really thought about it that way.

I was also thinking about your mother's vision—the one she had about the meaning of life when she gave birth to both you and Martin. In a way, your mother's vision has parallels to the garden story. I don't think you give your mother enough credit. Because if life is just like running on a hamster's wheel, the fact that humanity keeps trying actually makes us heroic and quite remarkable. You thought her vision meant that she believed that life was just effort going nowhere. But for her, I think, the message may have been that the meaning of life is not about the destination, but the journey and what you learn along the way.

And you think I've learned something from all the pain of this past year?

Yes, that it is okay for you to try your best, even if your best can't save others. As it is for God, sometimes it is enough to simply be broken-hearted when it's not within your power to save. In those times, you can just provide the support, if not the protection.

But how will I know when it's out of my power?

You know the serenity prayer, don't you?

Yes. "God, grant me the serenity to accept the things I cannot change, the courage to change the things I can, and wisdom to know the difference."

Pray for the wisdom.

And that will keep me from making all these mistakes?

No, Sya Meh. You can't avoid mistakes.

But why not?

Because there are no mistakes.

Acknowledgements

It would not have been possible to complete *First Mistake* without the generosity of so many who helped me tell my story in this unusual way. I owe a special debt of gratitude to the late, great Gordon Parks, who convinced me to throw out the initial draft of my first several chapters and start over by telling the story more simply and also to Gene Young who told me so many years ago that the most important thing is not to give up before I had finished. It has always been important to me to receive the feedback from my brother, who has always been my most important critic and creative partner. I am grateful to Tamim Ansary and the members of his memoir workshop who generously shared their stories and comments, helping me become a better writer and to keep making progress on the manuscript. The early readers of my first completed draft—my parents, Gene Young, Quandra Prettyman, Rosalind Whitehead, Rosemary Chang, Liane Larocque, and Debora Tully—provided me invaluable encouragement and feedback to help me improve what I had written. My friends on Facebook were incredibly kind to share with me their ideas for the updated subtitle and I'm especially indebted to Aaron Pike for the "winning" suggestion. And, finally, I'd like to thank Rob Kosberg, Lorna Walsh, and the whole Best Seller Publishing family for making the publication of *First Mistake* the fulfillment of a nearly quarter-century dream.

About the Author

D.J. Chang is a memoirist and social purpose entrepreneur. She now resides in the San Francisco Bay Area with her spouse and their dogs. D.J. was raised in a white, upper-middle-class suburb of New York City, where, as a child, she witnessed her caregiver die suddenly and, as a young adult, grappled with issues of sexuality, class, and ethnicity. Throughout her life, D.J. has searched for the meaning of identity, love, life, and death, and she explores these big questions and the events that shaped her life in her debut memoir, *First Mistake.*

CPSIA information can be obtained
at www.ICGtesting.com
Printed in the USA
FSHW01n1717090918
51936FS